Praise for
unfiltered

"Rachel Pedersen has much to teach us about how to start a business from nothing and grow it into an empire, because she speaks from experience—going from a single mom on food stamps to CEO of two multimillion-dollar companies. She knows firsthand all of the challenges and setbacks you will face and gives invaluable practical advice on how to overcome them. She will also teach you how to work magic with social media. This book is gold for aspiring entrepreneurs."

— **Robert Greene**, *New York Times* best-selling author of
The 48 Laws of Power

"Rachel is a truly heart-centered entrepreneur, and it shows in this book. Run, don't walk, to buy it, read it, and apply the invaluable wisdom in this book!"

— **Annie Grace**, best-selling author of *The Alcohol Experiment*

"Living in this digital world gives us all an opportunity to hide our true selves. We can filter our imperfections, delete our mistakes, and edit our real lives. Rachel is one of the few exceptions. Read her book and you'll be inspired. Apply it and you'll experience new business breakthroughs."

— **Kary Oberbrunner**, *Wall Street Journal* and *USA Today* best-selling author and CEO of Igniting Souls Publishing Agency

"The most modern, practical, and inspiring book available today for learning how to love yourself and your life as an entrepreneur. Herein you'll find everything you need to know about designing, envisioning, starting, and virally growing your biz or side hustle using the latest techniques and trends. Yes, you can do this, anyone can, and you're about to learn how."

— **Mike Dooley**, *New York Times* best-selling author of
Infinite Possibilities: The Art of Living Your Dreams

"Rachel is a legend in the making . . . and this book cements her status as someone who is knowledgeable but relatable. Her emotional anecdotes will take you on a wild journey, while her business advice is broken down beautifully with action steps. Bravo to this book and to Rachel!"

— **Amanda Holmes**, CEO of Chet Holmes International

"Unfiltered *is full of practical, hands-on advice for business owners and marketers alike. Rachel shares lessons that will save many business owners so much heartache, plus her stories will bring you on an emotional journey as you self-identify areas for growth in your business goals and dreams.*"

— **Chris Voss**, former FBI hostage negotiator, CEO and founder of *Black Swan Group,* and author of *Never Split the Difference*

"*Your future self will thank you for investing in this book. In* Unfiltered, *Rachel Pedersen offers up inspiration and intentional steps you can take to turn your dream into a real business.*"

— **Michael Stelzner**, founder of Social Media Examiner

"*Rachel is one of the most authentic, giving, and POWERFUL entrepreneurs I have ever met. She's an absolute force of nature and has impacted so many people for the better. The wisdom she shares is proven and actionable. When she speaks, I make it a point to listen. I recommend you do the same.*"

— **Kasim Aslam**, founder of Solutions 8

"*Rachel's growth is astonishing, and I have witnessed her becoming a powerhouse and a beacon of belief for those who want to do the same. She is committed to passing on that growth and development to all those around her! From single mom on welfare to a transformational leader . . . she pours her heart into everything she does, including this book!*"

— **Krista Mashore**, best-selling author and founder of Krista Mashore Coaching

"So many authors only show us the polished, shiny end result, making it hard to see how we could ever compare or achieve success. Rachel share insights and strategies while letting us in on the real raw journey. She has changed and grown so much since starting her business. Her growth is continually showcased as a beacon of possibility for her community members in everything that she does, including this powerful book!"

— **Molly Mahoney**, social media growth strategist (known as The Prepared Performer)

"Rachel Pedersen is one of the most authentic life-changing women I know, and this book is proof that we don't need to hide who we are or what our ambitions are; we don't need to fit a mold to make a real and massive impact."

— **Rachel Miller**, digital marketing strategist and specialist in social media organic growth

"In a world full of confusing business advice and gurus telling you who/how to be, Rachel cuts through the noise and delivers a powerful road map and instantly actionable steps based on proven paths and results. Don't walk, run to buy this book!"

— **Sarah Petty**, *New York Times* best-selling author of *Worth Every Penny*

"This book is a must-read for business owners, marketers, and freelancers."

— **Peng Joon**, author of *Build a Money Machine* and leading authority in wealth creation online

*"*Unfiltered *guides you to fully think through your entrepreneurial vision. The insight you gain from reading Rachel's book will serve you well—whether you are just getting started or needing to fine-tune what you are already doing to get better results. Being a business owner is a marathon and not a sprint, something that Rachel understands very well. This book will show you how to effectively communicate with clients, set clear expectations, and put in place what is needed to have a healthy work-life balance."*

— **Annie Hyman Pratt**, founder of Leading Edge Teams and author of *The People Part*

unfiltered

unfiltered

PROVEN STRATEGIES
TO START AND GROW YOUR BUSINESS
BY NOT FOLLOWING THE RULES

Rachel Pedersen

HAY HOUSE, INC.
Carlsbad, California • New York City
London • Sydney • New Delhi

Published in the United States by: Hay House, Inc.: www.hayhouse.com®
• *Published in Australia by:* Hay House Australia Pty. Ltd.: www.hayhouse
.com.au • *Published in the United Kingdom by:* Hay House UK, Ltd.:
www.hayhouse.co.uk • *Published in India by:* Hay House Publishers India: www.hayhouse.co.in

Cover design: Shubhani Sarkar • *Interior design:* Nick C. Welch
Indexer: Joan Shapiro

**Cataloging-in-Publication Data is on file
at the Library of Congress**

Hardcover ISBN: 978-1-4019-6751-2
E-book ISBN: 978-1-4019-6752-9
Audiobook ISBN: 978-1-4019-6817-5

10 9 8 7 6 5 4 3 2 1
1st edition, September 2022

Printed in the United States of America

SUSTAINABLE
FORESTRY
INITIATIVE
Certified Chain of Custody
Promoting Sustainable Forestry
www.sfiprogram.org
SFI-01268

SFI label applies to the text stock

To my kids:

My favorite role in this lifetime is not being "Rachel Pedersen," Rachel the author, Rach the businesswoman. My favorite role is being "Dakota's mom," "Delilah's mommy," and "Dominic's mother." I wrote this book to help pave the big, wonderful paths you will take in this world.

Contents

Foreword

"The life you want, the marriage you want, the family you want, will be fueled by the businesses you build."

I heard Garrett J. White say those words at our annual event, Funnel Hacking Live, and I remember looking out over the sea of people who were there, ready to start their entrepreneurial journey, and I remember wondering if they realized how the pursuit of their dreams would not only change their lives, but the lives of the people they had been called to serve.

A few weeks later, I had a meeting in Boise, Idaho, with my "Inner Circle." These are my high-end entrepreneurs who are the most committed to growing their companies. As we started the mastermind, I noticed a handful of new faces who had joined this exclusive mastermind group during the Funnel Hacking Live event a few weeks earlier. One of those faces was Rachel Pedersen.

I watched as she served the other entrepreneurs in the room, and how excited she would get every time she gave someone a shift that they could use, but I still didn't really know who she was.

A few hours later, it was her turn to come onstage and tell us her story. She told us a little about the struggles she had in her business and her life leading up to that point, and then she shared the story about the time that she "decided to go viral."

I noticed that she picked those words very carefully. It wasn't that she got lucky and something she created went viral. No, she *decided* . . . and then it happened.

This is something that you'll notice about Rachel. She's very intentional. As she told us her backstory and the struggles she had to overcome to be able to earn a seat in this room, I said to myself, "Oh my gosh, she's a Chain-Breaker!"

We see people who've been given a path, and that path defines them and becomes their chain, both for the good and for the bad. On both sides of that chain, rarely do you see people break their old situations, beliefs, or circumstances. But then there are those who magnificently and openly break those chains and choose to make their life happen.

From Rachel's resilient effort to create what she wanted, both her children's lives and countless other lives will be forever changed because of how she decided to rewrite her chains.

Of course, she's had the accolades of starting a business, going viral, enabling her husband to quit his 9-to-5 job, hiring teams of employees, and impacting untold lives. But she's done all this while at the same time being a mom.

So it's appropriate that when she sent me my first glimpse of this book, it was the cover—a picture worth a thousand words.

The first thing I see at the top is the Rachel I know, Rachel the entrepreneur—the one we constantly see online and the one we love.

But as you scan below, you see Rachel the mom—someone who sacrificed so much for her kids and for her family.

The cover says it all, because it shows the *reality* of life unfiltered.

Where most people are trying to show their life's highlight reels on social media, Rachel is willing to be vulnerable. She shows everyone exactly what it's actually like to be in business and to be a mom, to be successful and still feel the struggle, to have all of the ups and all of the downs each step of the way.

That is what this book is about.

My guess is you are looking to start a business, to change your life, to become somebody more than you are today. And my guess is that this is your personal calling: to become a Chain-Breaker; to change your future, not just for yourself, but for your family.

You have this moment with this book to make that commitment and make that change, and to do it in a way where you don't have to sacrifice who you are.

You can still be a mom or a dad and a business owner. You can be someone who's introverted or shy and is successful. You can be whatever you want to be. You never need to give up the life that you love to become who you are called to be and what you are capable of.

This book is going to teach you the business and life lessons to make sure that you can start a business and do it without compromising your ethics, your beliefs, and your values.

And show you how to do it in a way that's uniquely *you*.

As you start this journey with Rachel, I want you to realize that the pursuit of your entrepreneurial dreams will not only change your life and your family's life, but also the lives of the people you've been uniquely called to serve with your business.

Your business will become the fuel that will give you the life that you've been dreaming of! Be intentional and *decide* to create something amazing.

Russell Brunson, best-selling author
of *Dotcom Secrets*, *Expert Secrets*, and *Traffic Secrets*

Introduction

I woke up and immediately raced to my laptop.

It was June 2016, and I was in Memphis, Tennessee, looking to open a new franchise of the fast-food restaurant Mrs. Winner's Chicken & Biscuits, which was making a comeback after bankruptcy.

After weighing the options for funding the franchise, I landed on a wild and crazy idea: What if we crowdfunded the down payment, or even the total amount of the restaurant?

As far as I was concerned, the idea was an absolute winner—a winner winner chicken dinner, you might say. In the past six months, I had been doing research and learned that the Memphis market was craving Mrs. Winner's. After raising enough money and opening the franchise, my team would give back to the community with a huge party and free food.

Other people shared my excitement. Thanks to a press release about the crowdfunding idea, the story was picked up by tons of press in Tennessee. My team had also used Instagram to attract the attention of reporters. When my father and I handed out flyers about the campaign in barbershops, Baptist churches, businesses on Beale Street, and grocery stores, there was a strong positive response. In fact, the overall buzz about Mrs. Winner's was taking off. News about the campaign was blowing up on several different social media platforms. Everything seemed to be absolutely aligned.

So, that morning at my laptop, I had high hopes when I checked the newly launched campaign.

It was at $0.

Zero.

"That's okay, I just need to refresh the page," I told myself. I refreshed. And refreshed. And refreshed again. Only nothing was changing.

I wasn't panicking—yet. I was confident that today was going to be the first day of the rest of my life!

• • •

Less than a year before, my life had looked very different. I was working as a marketing manager at a network hardware company on the *Inc.* 5000. It was my first big corporate job. I really loved my coworkers and enjoyed the work I was doing.

However, the lack of schedule flexibility was difficult for me to navigate. I had started missing work occasionally for a variety of legitimate reasons. My kids would get sick, so I'd come in late. On other days, depression—something I've lived with for years—made it difficult for me to get out of bed, much less function in the office. After one of these instances, my direct boss wrote me up, which had never happened before.

Frustration crept up inside me. I felt terrible. But I feared that this scenario could have happened no matter where I worked—and it could happen again. Parents always have to juggle work and sick kids. I knew my depression wasn't going away. I thought, *Is this the forecast for the rest of my working life?* At the same time, I wasn't mad at the company or my boss. I was mad at myself. It wasn't about the job at all; I just wasn't where I wanted to be.

I had an idea, or more like a dream, bubbling up inside. I wanted to do something I felt passionate about on a schedule that worked for my family and me. I wanted to build my own business, focusing on helping others with social media marketing. But I had no idea where to start.

Then I discovered online communities for entrepreneurs and joined around 20 groups. Until then, I didn't realize building a business was so common. And even better, many people were doing it right from the comfort of their own home. I was blown away.

In November 2015, I officially started a side hustle while still working full-time at my day job. I began by moonlighting as a social media manager, using the skills I'd gained as a marketer to create, refine, and post content on social media such as Instagram and Facebook for a variety of clients, both brands and individuals. I mostly used LinkedIn and FB groups to secure my first clients, but I put my name in the hat for everything! Jobs, Craigslist gigs, tweets about companies hiring, and more. I was working on building my business whenever I could: before and after work, when the kids were in bed, during lunch breaks, and even on the toilet during bathroom breaks.

Things took off more quickly than I realized might be possible. By April 2016, I projected that my freelancing would generate $50,000 to $60,000 per year. Although I was terrified, I submitted my one-month notice at my 9-to-5.

One of my side gigs at the time was as a part-time marketing consultant for Mrs. Winner's. Not only did my friends John and Jeannie Buttolph own a franchise of the restaurant, but John was Mrs. Winner's CEO, and he was overseeing a reboot of the chain and brand after a 2010 bankruptcy.

Through them, I had the opportunity to learn about the profit margins on quick-serve food. I discovered that some fast-food fried chicken restaurants brought in $75,000 to $90,000 per year in profit. *Profit!* And the top-performing restaurants—which of course we would be—brought in $150,000.

I started to do the math and very quickly realized that if we built restaurant after restaurant, we could make a goal of opening 10 restaurants. With 10 restaurants opened in a decade or less, we would be making between $750,000 and $1,500,000 per year in profit. All from fried chicken!

It was a yes from me.

In spring 2016, my husband, Poul, and I presented the idea to John. I told him that food lovers in Memphis absolutely loved (and were asking for) Mrs. Winner's. When he pulled out the past records of stores in Memphis, he found those stores had indeed performed extremely well.

It's hard to get approved for franchise ownership, but John gave me his blessing to open a Memphis store myself if I could fund the restaurant. I already knew my dad was on board as restaurant manager. After doing all the research—*cough cough*, googling the cost for opening a fast-food restaurant and downloading premade business plans—I calculated it was going to cost somewhere between $250,000 and $350,000 to open the restaurant.

Sign me up! I know how to bargain shop like no one's business—I bet I could do it for $150,000.

Now it was time to get the funding in place. We met with a banker who specialized in small business association (SBA) loans, and I shared my research and business plan. Unfortunately, the bank's owner started asking me some really important questions I had overlooked in the research process.

Owner: So, you live in Minnesota and want to open a new Mrs. Winner's Chicken and Biscuits restaurant in Memphis?

Me: Yes!

Owner: Well, we would need you to live near the restaurant to handle problems.

Me, *quickly and thinking on my feet*: My husband and dad can take turns flying down to Memphis to take care of the restaurant.

Owner: How are you going to pay for that?

Me: The profits would take care of that! And we could rent an apartment in Memphis for them to live in every other week.

Owner: How much money are you asking for?

Me: $150,000 to $250,000.

Owner: That's a lot of money to ask for a first-time loan, but I think we can do that. How much do you have for the down payment?

Me: The what?

Owner: The down payment.

Me, *figuring I could find a way to scrounge up a couple thousand dollars*: How much is a down payment usually for this type of loan?

Owner: $40,000 to $50,000.

Me: I'm going to need a couple of days.

In my heart, I knew the truth. Our credit was in the 500s. We had $29 in our savings account. And we had absolutely no way of generating $50,000 in the next few months.

But still, I wasn't ready to give up. I applied for grants, loans, bridge lending, angel investments—every opportunity I could think of. I applied for *Shark Tank*. We even asked for a $50K loan from Poul's uncle, a famous architect—who said he respected my boldness, but the investment wasn't a good fit for him at the time. And to top it off, John was applying pressure, letting me know he needed a timeline for this restaurant's opening.

That's when I had my crowdfunding idea. We already knew that the public wanted Mrs. Winner's, so I was positive we could create a highly visible campaign that would have donations pouring in to finance the down payment.

This was going to work, I knew it! I had previously managed some social media for crowdfunding campaigns, so I knew what kind of work they entailed. We picked a date for the launch. Poul and I had one credit card with a little room available for charging, so we printed flyers with the website for the campaign, built a marketing funnel to secure e-mail addresses, and produced a video. John was also supportive of this crowdfunding idea and helped spread the word.

When the weekend of the crowdfunding launch arrived, my dad and I flew down to Memphis. Strangely, I had this weird, sinking feeling in my stomach when the plane took off. Something wasn't feeling right, and I didn't know how to explain it. However, I brushed off my doubts and got down to work promoting the campaign.

Little did I know that I should have trusted my gut.

The campaign was set to go live at noon, and my dad and I spent the morning handing out promotional flyers.

Noon came and went. The press we had arranged went live. As I hoped, our crowdfunding campaign now had more than $0, but not much more. We had only about $150 in backers—$115 of which was from us, spent on our credit card.

My heart sank.

Our campaign wasn't taking off. It wasn't going viral. We weren't going to be fully backed.

I still remember the horrible feeling of facing my dad and updating him every time he asked, "How's the campaign doing?" I remember the dread I felt at the thought of calling Poul and telling him that I had failed to fulfill his belief in me, that I hadn't pulled through for our family and our future.

Good-bye, Mrs. Winner's Chicken and Biscuits franchise owner plans. Hello, harsh reality.

I was so embarrassed to have let so many people down.

I was embarrassed I let my husband down.

I was embarrassed that my dad was there—he'd flown to Memphis on his own dime—and I was letting him down.

I was embarrassed I let down the franchise.

I was embarrassed that we had faced Poul's uncle and asked for money, and it hadn't worked.

I was embarrassed to face John and Jeannie Buttolph, who had believed in me.

Plus, I was mortified knowing that everyone was watching me fail publicly. I'd shared the campaign enthusiastically on social media and with friends—I'd put it *everywhere*, with no filter. So many people reached out afterward and were like, "When are you opening the restaurant?" That made me want to crawl into a hole of shame. It felt too transparent, like I was undressing in public.

Now, it's scary to live in an unfiltered way in front of others, even people we trust. Baring our dreams, deepest wishes, and expectations can expose our biggest insecurities and shortcomings. But what I didn't know then was that in business, taking off the filters can be a positive thing. Every single layer that you peel back reveals new things about who you are, and both your successes and mistakes become lessons along the way.

Yet I had fallen into a common trap. Business owners are often reluctant to embrace vulnerability. Instead, they create this illusion that their business is totally polished—in other words, everything is running smoothly and going great—when the unfiltered truth is anything but.

When we don't allow ourselves to face our insecurities, it can be a shock when suddenly someone finds out the truth and sees everything we haven't shared. It's beyond undressing in public; it's more like being fully naked. And we realize, *Well, now I'm not just visible—I'm being seen without any filters, and my business is all out there.*

That was me in that Memphis hotel room. I was totally vulnerable and exposed. Every mistake I made was out there for everyone to see. My dad and Poul both told me how proud they were of me, but I felt like they were just saying that. I wanted to fall apart and disappear; I was so humiliated. I literally lay down on the hotel floor and said, "Hey, Dad, I love you. But you're not going to be able to say anything that makes me feel better right now."

I grieved; that's the best word for it. It was pretty ugly.

I bawled my eyes out for hours. I sobbed. A big, foggy cloud of depression came over me. It felt like the deepest, darkest hole I'd ever been in. It wasn't the deepest, darkest thing I'd ever gone through—but to me, it was everything that the campaign represented, like saying good-bye to the 9-to-5 and hello to working on my own terms. I had put my dream on the line, in front of everyone. And I'd failed.

On top of all that, I had also started making a ton of mistakes on one of my other client's social media accounts. I kept misspelling "entrepreneur," and, soon after, they let me go. Suddenly, I was like, *I don't know if I can do this. I think I need to find a job. There is no way I can be responsible for running a company. I lost another big client. I messed up; I let everyone down.*

Eventually, I stopped crying. I ended up having an amazing conversation with my dad in that hotel room, and it felt like at least one good thing had come out of that horrible situation. And I was like, *Okay. I can keep going just a little bit more.* Poul, my dad, and I were able to pick ourselves up. I got my money back from the crowdfunding. And when I got home, I saw that a new client had signed up to work with me.

In the moment, it didn't feel like I had bounced back at all. But in hindsight, I realized how much of that Mrs. Winner's failure was related to perception. We think that when failure happens, the entire world knows about it. It's that whole fishbowl syndrome—thinking that anyone can see anything you do at any moment. But not everybody knew I had failed—or saw me fail so publicly. And it didn't diminish my worth as a person or professional. The truth is, everything was fine, and life went on—and I went on.

Today, I'm the founder and CEO of RBP Productions, which encompasses a digital marketing agency, provides social media and digital strategy to clients, and works with entrepreneurs to help them grow their own businesses. In fact, RBP Productions was named one of the *Inc.* 5000 fastest-growing companies in the Midwest in 2020. I've also won multiple Two Comma Club awards, which you receive for generating $1 million from a single ClickFunnels sales funnel.

From creating and posting hundreds of videos about all aspects of marketing and social media strategy, I grew my online audience, which now includes more than a million TikTok followers. I also received a Silver Creator Award for 100,000 subscribers on YouTube. I have met and even been mentored by some of my heroes. Because of all this, Poul and I have been able to pay off our debts, buy our dream home, and build a studio for our business. I'm also able to give back: every month, we donate to nonprofits or charities.

It's safe to say I've come a long way since I was a single mom on assistance, drowning in debt and working night and day to make ends meet and create a better life for my family.

WHY THIS IS THE BUSINESS BOOK FOR YOU

The truth is, starting a business is one of the top five hardest decisions I've made in my life. In the beginning, I thought to myself, *Once I make a six-figure income, I will have made it! All my problems will be gone, we will be making bank, I'll be living my best life!* So I sprinted to six figures as quickly as humanly possible. Of course, my problems didn't go away once I reached that milestone. It doesn't become easier just because your business is bigger; the challenges just become bigger as well. Every single day, I'm still presented with setbacks, challenges, oppositions, and doubts. But what I can say is this: it does become second nature to keep moving forward.

And I've learned that you can't find solutions to your problems if you aren't willing to face them. Sure, it can be nerve-racking to be transparent and honest about the bajillion things that go wrong every single day—the difficulties, mistakes, insecurities, and flat-out failures. Sure, there are times when I just want to hide. But I've found that if I peel back a layer, undress a little bit, and go to people I trust, I find great solutions.

If you're reading this book, maybe you're preparing to take the first step toward starting a business of your own. Perhaps you're interested in taking your existing small business to the next level. In either case, chances are you're facing some hard decisions, just as I was. My hope is that this book will inspire and guide you on your business growth journey and provide you wisdom and best practices gleaned from my own trial and error that you can return to time and time again.

I've divided *Unfiltered* into four parts. At the end of each chapter, I provide simple, actionable takeaways—prompts for journaling, ideas to reflect on and use as encouragement when days are hard, and easy steps to implement into your life or business plans right away.

Part One shares advice on how you can determine and nurture your purpose. This includes practical strategies for figuring out what kind of business you want to start and uses real-life examples from my own experience and history. We'll lay the groundwork for growth, illustrate best practices for any kind of entrepreneur, and provide insights to set your launch up for success.

In Part Two, I detail how I approach social media and digital marketing strategy and help you think about the best ways to embrace these important elements and effectively incorporate them into your growing business so that you see results.

Part Three focuses on actionable ways to position a business for profit. I outline what I call business-by-design—a straightforward guide you can use to cultivate solid boundaries and good business habits; define how you work and communicate with clients; and establish essential practices. I share some real-life examples of what went right (and wrong!) with clients as I built my business, and I talk about the importance of building a solid circle of support via mentors and your network.

Part Four offers advice for hanging on when your journey becomes an emotional roller coaster. It's also all about the surprising things I've learned—and how I've reacted in response. I offer strategies for creating a unique road map so you can find your own way to get ahead without sacrificing the things that matter most. There is also advice on maintaining your personal passion and finding ways to recapture it if it gets lost.

The very fact that you're reading this book tells me that maybe time is a rare and valuable resource in your life.

Maybe you're thinking, *Rachel, time isn't just valuable—it's slipping through my hands. I can't freaking catch up.* Maybe you're in a season of life where you're up at all hours with a toddler who won't sleep through the night. Maybe you're in the season of life where your teen's activities have you running all over town. Or maybe you're in a season of life where your job is working you into the ground. Maybe you spent the only "fun money" you have on this book. (Holy moly, if that's the case, let's make this book the best investment you've ever made.) Maybe you had your hopes dashed in the past and you're barely clinging to your dream.

No matter the reason, what's most important is that you're here and choosing to embrace hope. The first steps toward your dream are the hardest, and I hope the strategies in this book will support you as you begin that journey. But I also believe what I share can help you build a foundation that will last you through many more seasons—of business and of life. I'm absolutely honored you're here, reading this book and sharing your incredibly important dreams with me.

PART I

PURPOSE

CHAPTER 1

Why Are You Starting a Business?

Ask a hundred people to tell you their journey of starting a business, and you'll get a hundred different answers. Your upbringing, interests, personal challenges, and available opportunities all combine to inform the business you choose to start. But why do you want to do it in the first place? Figuring out your why for starting a business is difficult partly because this reason will change throughout your life. When I began freelancing in 2015, I had different responsibilities than when I was 18 and working as a restaurant host in the Mall of America. I was a completely different person at a different stage of life.

One thing to know is that every experience can be applied toward your next opportunity. Thanks to that restaurant job, I landed a management internship through Lettuce Entertain You Enterprises, a well-known Midwest restaurant company. I was fascinated by how confident the managers at the restaurant were. It seemed as though they always knew exactly what was going on, and one day, I wanted to have that level of certainty. Plus, I thought that learning how to run a restaurant would be good preparation for owning one someday.

Only two people across all of Minnesota won this internship, but the other intern was kicked out of the program. So I ended up representing the entire state. As part of the internship, I shadowed the management of another restaurant and learned a ton—how to staff, prep, document, and open and close the restaurant. I also created a mock restaurant plan and concept, which involved, among other things, calling supply places to find out how much booths, cups, and menus cost. It was really a fantastic experience.

At the end of the internship, they flew everyone in the program to Chicago to present their business ideas to the founder of Lettuce Entertain You. Now, every other intern presented in big groups of 3, 5, or 10 people. But I was alone—it was just me, discussing the Mediterranean-style restaurant I alone had developed. The founder told me, "Everyone else had people to work with, and you're the only one who was here by yourself. I'm really, really impressed by that." When I look back now, that was first time I thought starting a business might be something I not only wanted to do but could someday accomplish. Though it took me a while to get there, that's not uncommon. There's no perfect time to start a business, and it's never too late to make that choice. As your life priorities change, new career paths often reveal themselves when you least expect them.

START YOUR FIRE

When you're trying to make a fire, there are different types of wood you can use. You can imagine the different whys—the reasons for beginning your business—as different kinds of fire starters. First up, there's kindling, which is small twigs or other material that easily catch fire. This option offers a very strong fire starter that gets things going quickly. Kindling is necessary, but it burns really fast and disappears just as quickly. It is the equivalent of your reason being *I need money now.* Though it may be true—I know I've been there—a shortsighted, quick-burning reason doesn't leave a lot of room for passion or introspection or mistakes. In the long run, the business will fizzle out.

The second fire starter you might try are sticks. These are pretty easy to gather and will last a little bit longer because they have more structure. This wood represents your personal reasons for wanting to start a business, such as *I want more time for myself or to provide a better life for my children.* These reasons are important—they are close to your heart

The third and final fire starter are logs. Logs might be heavier, taking more effort to gather and longer to catch fire, but they can burn for hours. Once they get going, you don't have to keep constantly running out to find more fuel; you can just enjoy the warmth of the fire. Logs represent commitment to a purpose bigger than yourself such as wanting to help others or create positive change in your community, certain systems, or the world.

When I left my steady marketing job in 2016, my main why was because I didn't want my life to pause for someone else's dream. I wanted to be able to work from home and take care of my kids when they were sick or leave early if they needed rides to their after-school activities. I wanted to do things at my own pace if my depression flared up or skip work if I needed a mental health day without fearing repercussions. I saw that the company's founder had that flexibility, often leaving work early or taking Fridays off. But how could I get there too?

Connecting with members of online communities for entrepreneurs opened my eyes—that path was available to me if I could run my own business successfully. People discussed what worked and didn't work and asked each other, "How do I do this?" or "What happened when you tried that?" One day I finally said, *Wait a second—I am sitting here working for someone else every day. I don't want to sit here and build someone else's dreams. That's it. I'm building my own business.*

In recent years, I randomly ran into the owner of that network hardware company on a flight, and we caught up. It was really nice to see him. He told me, "I see you from time to time on social media, and I'm really proud of you." That made me feel good—and made me realize I had made the right decision.

What's Your Why?

Finding your why is crucial for your business to succeed. A great way to start thinking about this is to write it down. Grab a pen and paper and journal some reasons—there's no right or wrong. This is something you can revisit and refine as you develop your plan. For example, you might want:

- To spend more time with family

- The ability to support friends/family

- To not worry about basic physical needs like food, shelter, or security

- To be successful

- To join a welcoming community

- To use and refine your creative talents

- To be your own boss

- To feel empowered and self-fulfilled

FIND YOUR SQUARE ONE

Deciding to take that leap and starting a business is one thing. Getting out of your own way and launching a business is another thing entirely.

When I began to grow my social media business, feelings that I was a total fraud immediately took over. A gigantic *Imposter!* sign started flashing in my brain. What if everyone finds out that:

- I don't have a degree.
- I'm a fun-loving, goofy, bubbly blonde.
- I don't have the pedigree or background for business.

Every single day, the list of all the reasons I had no business starting a business filled my head. Maybe some of these sound familiar to you:

- I don't know how to follow a budget.
- I don't get spreadsheets.
- I'm not great at communicating.
- I'm super disorganized.
- I can be very emotional.
- I don't have a safety net of savings.
- I have bad credit and can't secure loans or financing.
- I have two kids (at the time; now I have more!).
- I'm not the smartest person in the room.

And, above all, I had *absolutely no idea* how to build a business. Of course, nobody does at first. With this negativity growing all the time, I knew I needed to make a list of all the reasons I should start a business—and why I was the best person to start that business. I sat down with my journal and my Papermate pens, and after an hour, I only came up with two reasons, which weren't even that great or original:

1.   Because I have a dream.
2.   Because I'm the only me.

I still didn't know what building a business looked like, and I had no idea how I was going to start.

If this describes you, identifying why you want to start a business is a good first step. Next, you need to figure out what kind of business makes sense for your life. I call this finding your square one. Different personality types are suited to different types of businesses. Plus, not every business will fit everyone's lifestyle—and not every season makes sense for you to start a business. In other words, every business is going to look different, not just in its actual model, but also in the way that it's run, from the top on down.

For example, I'm not meant to work for someone else and have a boss. I realized being in an office where I must report in from 9 to 5, Monday through Friday, wasn't for me. And, in hindsight, I realize now that I'm not exactly the best employee in the world—I'm much better managing my own time and work.

Think of it as though you're comparing different places you could live. Living in New York is very different from living in Iowa; living in California is very different from living in Texas. Although you can have a happy family and house in any of those places, they're all going to have very different feels. Comparatively, you also are going to a very different lifestyle living in Santa Fe, Greece, or Costa Rica.

You must look for the indications that a particular location is one where you could live. But to get an idea for what things are going to be like, you need to do research. For example, I personally couldn't live in Iowa. I need a big city with lots of shopping options, and I need all my stores nearby. Now, I don't have to move to Iowa to learn this; I've talked to enough people who live there already to know that.

However, you could also say that New York sounds fantastic. But you won't know if you love the city until you visit it, learn about it or watch movies about it. When you get there, you might be like, "This is really different than what I expected."

You have to be super honest that there are going to be pros and cons to every single location—just like there are going to be pros and cons to every single type of business. One of the things you're going to want to do is talk to people, ask questions, and learn about different business models.

Here are a few things that will help you find your square one.

Start with Passion

Take inventory of what lights you up. The more passionate you are about something, the more you are willing to work for it. My interests include reading, learning languages, traveling, talking, and playing games with friends. Are you seeing a pattern here? I love learning and communication! Social media was a no-brainer for me, though I first fell in love with the online world because of all the possibilities it offered. Anyone from anywhere can connect with anyone from anywhere. So if you think, *I don't have the opportunity or network* or *My city doesn't have this,* social media suddenly opens that up. I started actively using social media while living in Anoka, Minnesota. If I can connect with big Hollywood names from Anoka—and I did!—you can find the connections you need. That's really cool to me.

Uncover Your Hidden Superpowers

Look at the kryptonite from your past—a.k.a. the things that others thought were your weaknesses. In reality, there are superpowers hidden inside these weaknesses. For example, teachers always wrote on my grade school report cards, "Rachel is way too social. She talks too much and is a distraction in class." Now, however, I'm the Queen of Social Media because those shortcomings are actually skills that make me a perfect social media manager. I love communicating. I love getting a message across to people and packaging something in a fun way. I love having fun and being creative. Plus, I love getting attention, so it always feels good when you see engagement on social media. And I love taking a challenge and solving it.

Try Everything

We assume that we need to have our life's trajectory figured out in the first four years of being an adult—like, by our early 20s. But the truth is, what if it took you eight years to find something you could love doing for the rest of your life? Wouldn't that be worth the wait? If you can't figure out what you want to do, give yourself a month to try this, or a month to try that, or even a year to try each one. From the outside, businesses can be deceiving. For example, sometimes people think that starting a brick-and-mortar boutique, with lots of influencers, will be fantastic. And then they discover that it's not as glamorous as it looks. If you don't have the resources to drop everything and commit a lot of time to something you're uncertain about, you can interview people who have tried those things or do a trial run by working at a similar business.

Find a Compatible Mentor

Mentors offer an invaluable wealth of knowledge. Find a mentor who has achieved something similar to your goals and whose values and morals align with yours, and look into what they suggest or recommend. Always feel free to get a second opinion from another mentor you trust. The key in finding a mentor is making sure that they've achieved something similar to what you want to do in terms of success. We'll go into more depth about that in a later chapter.

Create a Vision Board

Vision boards can be just about anything you want, and they offer a visual and more tactile representation of your why. There are several ways to vision-board, including:

- Create a list with pen and paper and put it in a place you'll regularly see it, such as on your bedside table or by the mirror in your bathroom.

- Get a small whiteboard to write your list on so you can continually add to, change, or annotate your vision.

- Collect images and words from magazines or other sources and paste them onto a big poster board.

- Go digital and create a Pinterest board.

I started my first vision board (using a whiteboard) in the fall of 2015. I was moved to do this because many people I considered role models—Oprah, Reese Witherspoon, Celine Dion, Meryl Streep, Shonda Rhimes, Deepak Chopra—kept mentioning them. Over and over, they all talked about the power of visualizing their goals, and how vision boards helped them achieve that.

Vision boards don't have to be confined to just your business goals—dream big! For example, on my vision board, I included a wish for a house with a really beautiful grand staircase and two-story ceilings. Why is that? It's not because I actually needed a staircase. To me, the staircase represented a future where I could line my kids up on the steps to take their pictures before prom. The tall ceilings represented the ability to have my whole, huge family over for the holidays with a Christmas tree big enough that we could fit everyone's presents underneath it. And now, reader, I have my gorgeous dream house. It has two-story ceilings. We can have everyone over for game night thanks to a basement that fits a ton of people. I love celebrating Christmas at home because all of our nieces and nephews fit in the house. And when my kids go to prom, they're going to line up on the stairs—count on it.

Tips to Get Started

Use these questions as a guide to start dreaming up your vision board. Nothing is stupid or off limits. Nothing even needs to make sense yet. Just start dreaming!

- What do I want to do every day?
- What do I want to see, smell, and hear?
- What sorts of environments am I most comfortable in?

- What lights me up?

- What is the best—or my favorite—version of myself?

- How can I be a role model?

- If everything on my vision board came true, would I feel as though I had dreamed big enough?

- If I knew I couldn't fail, what would I add to my vision board?

- What would make my younger self proud?

- How do I want my obituary to read?

- Will this inspire the next generation?

HOW DO YOU DEFINE SUCCESS?

As you figure out the kind of business you want to grow, you're also going to learn how you define success. By typical external milestones—clients, revenue, partnerships—my business is a success. However, I long ago realized that my definition of a successful business is more personal. It's not about the appearance or perception of success as measured by someone else's definition. It's about building a business that aligns with what I want from life and helps other people get what they want as well. That can mean many different things. It might mean a business that employs people in a healthy way and serves customers well. It might mean a business that has a positive impact and empowers all the people it touches. Owners see profit, but the business also grows at the right pace and gives back.

When I was growing up, my grandmother and aunt both ran their own businesses. Like many kids, I didn't really understand what they did—or how hard they worked—until I was older.

I remember that my grandmother was always sewing. But I had no idea she was a well-known seamstress and designer. She had clients from China, and they would fly in or she would fly to them for fittings so she could create custom suits and dresses. As family legend goes, she even taught the legendary restaurateur Leeann Chin how to sew. (Yes, that Leeann Chin!) My aunt, meanwhile, owned a ballet studio. Her students were mostly kids, but she also taught select adults. She and my cousin sometimes lived in her ballet studio or in their car—a fact I value now because I realize she ate, slept, and breathed her business. It was that important to her, and I relate to her dedication.

Now, neither my aunt nor my grandmother was rich. They didn't resemble the business owners I later learned about in *Inc.* or *Forbes*. But both built thriving businesses back before entrepreneurship was a popular thing. And, more importantly, they both loved what they did. They're both examples of the idea that there's no wrong kind of business to start—and no wrong way to start a business.

The main thing to remember is that success looks different for everyone. And, as your business grows and changes, your definition of success will also evolve. Mistakes will happen along the way no matter how prepared you are—I've made my fair share! But being able to clearly say what your aims are for starting your business and being willing to do research (more on that in the next chapter!) will set you up for a success that's *your* success—not anyone else's.

TAKEAWAYS

- *Journal:* There are many reasons you might want to start a business—independence, flexibility, money, following your passion—and this reason is often different at different stages of your life. As you begin your journey, it's important to find your why. Grab your journal and check out the sidebar on page 6 for more ideas.

- *Reflect:* What does success look like to you? Your version of success is probably not going to be the same as someone else's. Understanding the way you want to be successful shows you what you're bringing to the table—and it'll help squash that imposter syndrome too.

- *Do:* Create a vision board. I cannot stress enough the importance of visualizing your dreams being part of actualizing them. Flip to page 11 for more ideas on how to get started.

CHAPTER 2

Research, Research, Research

If you're reading this book, you're probably feeling unfulfilled at your job. Or maybe you aren't working at the moment. Either way, you want more and you know you have more to offer. Maybe you've tried climbing the corporate ladder, but you're stuck or perhaps just feeling uninspired.

Why not build your own ladder? That's the choice I made.

The Different Types of Business Owners

At first, your business goals may be monetary ones. That's totally fine, because metrics such as revenue and profits are familiar to us, so it's easier to plan strategies to reach these milestones.

In fact, one helpful way you can look at business growth and ownership is via the different revenue thresholds: a five-figure, six-figure, or seven-figure business owner.

The principles of business by design apply no matter what level you're at, but businesses on each of these levels operate slightly differently. So let's look at five- and six-figure businesses. We'll talk about seven-figure business owners later in the book (see Chapter 21).

Generally speaking, five- and six-figure business owners require similar skill sets. Both run their own businesses by themselves—without them, the business wouldn't exist. The five-figure business owner is really and truly a freelancer. This means that they can usually work the hours that they want, but they are working for someone. Often, freelancers still have day jobs. They take on jobs from multiple clients, even simultaneously. But the client is the one who has control over the finished product. A six-figure business owner, sometimes called a solopreneur, is referred to as self-employed. This means they choose what they're working on, when, and how much. They have customers who are seeking their products or services. They might even hire freelancers or other employees.

WHERE TO START

If you've mentioned to anyone your aim to start a business, you've probably already gotten lots of advice about what to study or research. For example, many experts recommend creating business plans. Though these can give you an idea of what you're in for, business plans are just guesses and projections. They're like the weather: you never truly know what's going to happen. The truth is that nothing quite prepares you for running a business like running a business. That's why I recommend starting with these points.

1. Explore the Barriers to Entry

Part of the reason I became a freelancer is because there's minimal to no barrier to entry. This means there are few obstacles that prevent just about anyone from entering the industry. You do not need experience or a degree to get started in most of the online freelancing space. It can cost you close to nothing, besides maybe a little bit of business paperwork. And you don't have to invest much, if anything, at first. You don't need a logo, a portfolio, or even a website. The basics you will need are a computer and Internet access, though there might be other minimal requirements depending on your industry. The good news is that, after saving a percentage of money for taxes, the rest of your business can be profit. When I started making money freelancing, very little of it was spent on anything for the business besides a couple of tools that I wanted to make my job easier.

One of the only barriers to entry for freelancing might be time. Successful freelancing depends on how much you're willing or able to work, especially in the beginning. If you don't have much experience, you might be doing more work for less money—but just remember that all experience is good experience. As you refine skills and make connections, you'll be able to charge more and work less.

2. Define the Foundational Aspects

The most important part of any structure is the foundation. To make something that will last, you have to build it from the ground up—so start with the foundational aspects. To figure this out, you want to ask yourself questions like:

- How much is this going to cost?
- For every dollar I make, how many cents am I going to bring home?

- What are the costs of goods?
- If this doesn't work, what can the pivot look like?
- Is this something that's not easy to pivot?
- Is this a model I can get behind?

Starting to figure out your niche—and audience—is also part of this process. I ended up starting my podcast *Social Media Secrets* because I was looking for a podcast that talked frankly about how to best use social media hosted by someone like me, and I couldn't find one. Today we have over 500,000 downloads.

My podcast is successful because I talk about a variety of topics—but it's bite-size. Episodes run 5–15 minutes, and we produce them several times per week. I know that my audience doesn't have time for 60-minute episodes. They also don't have time to sit down and listen to tons of podcasts. They're listening in the carpool. They're listening while they're making dinner or walking the dog. Bite-size works.

3. Study the Attributes of Leaders

My favorite topic to study is leadership. Good leaders take ownership, communicate, and commit to moving forward. They are also honest and continually working on themselves. They do hard things, they're disciplined, and they lead by example. I knew I wanted to be one of these leaders. So I started listening to podcasts, reading books, finding interviews online—anything that I could to hear more from the people I looked up to.

There was a point in my life when I was working 50–60 hours a week and I didn't have money for extra expenses or even a lot of time to read. But I knew that reading was important because I'd heard so many podcasts and interviews with successful people talking about how reading changed their lives.

So on weekends when I didn't work, I'd spend some time reading lists online such as "top business books," "leadership books," "communication books," and "personal growth books." And then I would take screenshots of the lists, pack up my oldest, and go to Goodwill. I would scour the shelves, especially on special discount days when books would be $1 each or even 10 for $1. One of the most powerful books I ever read, *The Millionaire Next Door*, I found at Goodwill for a quarter. I still have the book with the price sticker on it! I read books from all the people who created the success I want to achieve. Before I ever hired Russell Brunson as my mentor, I read his first book, *Dotcom Secrets*, twice.

Of course, you might never have the opportunity or means to spend time with someone you look up to. For example, I don't get to hang out with Brené Brown or Shonda Rhimes, but reading their books is a relatively inexpensive way to have their full attention and expertise. Even if I met any of my heroes, I wouldn't have tons of time to ask all the questions I've ever wanted to ask. But through the pages of their book, you get to spend many hours with them, and you can take what you learn and apply it to your own situation.

Reading can become your free mentor for all the seasons of your life.

Easy Ways to Get Books Cheap or for Free

- Public library
- Trading with friends
- Certain YouTube channels

- Online media sites such as Google Books, Open Culture, Open Library, Project Gutenberg, Z-Library
- Library of Congress
- Scribd or Audible
- Kindle
- Used local bookstores
- Used on Amazon, Book Depository, Thrift-Books, or other online retailers
- Secondhand/thrift stores
- Garage/estate sales

EVERYTHING CAN BE RESEARCH

Research and analysis are key for business growth. And, of course, there are times when you will have to make a business plan. After my Mrs. Winner's snafu, if I needed to create a profitable and effective business or marketing plan in six weeks, I would research for four weeks before making a single move.

I learned how to be nimble and curious from my dad. When I was a kid, he always said, "If you don't have the money, you better have the time." That's stuck with me my whole life. Any time someone asked me, "Can you figure this out?" I'd be like, "Yeah, totally, I can." And then I would go and search online until I found the answers. Later in life, this advice helped me learn how to be resourceful: to find answers, to find mentors, to find the books, to find YouTube videos, anything. We all have the time and ability to do research, even just by looking at what's around us. You can see the world as a teacher. In fact, the world is offering you a crash course on business, marketing, and communication.

That mailer pack filled with coupons? That's no ordinary junk mail. This is a curriculum: what lines, words, images, and colors grab your attention? As you scroll through TikTok or YouTube, notice what kind of content compels you to click. What are the titles? What do the thumbnails look like?

Next, it's time to start taking screenshots of all the advertising and marketing you are noticing. On your computer or phone, create a folder of these screenshots and take note of the patterns that emerge. This can tell an entire story of what works well in business and marketing. If you can't take photos or screenshots, jot down notes about what you see. I personally love to create these kinds of files, and I'm almost always collecting research in this way while I'm on social media or anywhere else I see or hear something interesting.

You too can start researching everything and everywhere in your world. Here's a list of some of my favorite research-in-the-wild resources and, best of all, they are all inexpensive or already exist in your environment, free of charge.

- Commercials on TV
- Netflix thumbnails
- Movie trailers
- Posts on social media that go viral
- TikTok videos
- Facebook ads
- YouTube thumbnails and video titles
- Twitter trends
- Instagram's explore page

- Pinterest pins
- Online forums (Reddit is amazing for studying people/problems)
- E-mail subject lines—I sign up for every news-letter I can just to study subject lines
- E-mail contents (sales *and* nonsales)
- Ads on websites
- Blog titles
- Book covers
- Junk mail
- Billboards
- Bus stop advertisements
- Magazine advertisements
- Window displays
- Posters in classrooms, doctors' offices, grocery stores
- T-shirt slogans

Here's what you should look for:

1. What seems to be working well?
2. What's getting engagement?
3. What are the patterns?
4. What flopped massively?

Everything is an opportunity for learning. The world is your oyster when you see everything as an opportunity to study business and marketing. And remember, you can learn as much from things that fail as you can from those that succeed.

If you want to become an influencer . . . start with research.
If you want to start a business . . . start with research.
If you want to become a marketer . . . start with research.

TAKEAWAYS

- *Journal:* Consider what the foundational aspects of your business will look like. What will things cost? Who do you want your audience to be? If you aren't sure, then what kind of research do you need to do to find out?

- *Reflect:* Choose a day that you can take note, throughout the day, of all the marketing you are exposed to. Once you have your list, take some time to consider what stuck with you and what you forgot. Think about the patterns you see in effective marketing.

- *Do:* Find a book by someone who inspires you or on a topic that relates to your business—whether at a bookstore, library, or online—and get reading!

CHAPTER 3

Programming Your Mind for Success

The first step of being a business owner is getting into the mindset of a business owner. And you can't get into the mindset of someone without spending time with them. For example, say someone had never spent time with kids before becoming a parent. Chances are, they would have a difficult time getting into the mindset of what a kid wants or needs.

The same is true with business. You need to be around people who are also building businesses, so that you have a place that feels like your safe place to share wins, lows, and vulnerable things, and ask for support. All of these are so important. However, business owners are busy—and you probably are too—so what's the best way to be around them? If you read Chapter 2, you're probably already doing it. I read books, listened to podcasts, and watched YouTube videos and a ton of *Shark Tank*. These things all helped me get a sense of how business owners communicated and presented themselves, which was priceless for understanding and being able to replicate their mindset.

A hard truth to learn is that traditional school doesn't necessarily set you up for success when it comes to business ownership. So in order to change your mindset, you have to reprogram yourself for entrepreneurship. For me, this means spending at least 10 to 15 minutes every single morning preparing my mind before I start the workday. I meditate, do visualization exercises, journal about what I want to achieve, and use positive- and success-based affirmations. This mental preparation is an intentional process that you have to work on every day. Your mindset is like the foundation for a house. You can build the same exact house on a good foundation and a bad foundation—and only one of them is going to last. The same thing is true with your mindset.

PROBLEM VERSUS CHALLENGE MINDSET

At a traditional job, you've probably experienced a problem mindset. When there's an issue with something, you bring it to your boss or team and it gets decided on or sorted out (or not) through a myriad of processes. But when you're a business owner, there's no one to bring your problems to—it's all on you to find the solution.

It may seem simple, but one way to reframe the problem mindset is to change how you word things, from "I've got a problem" to "We've got a challenge." "Problem" presents more of a barrier, a closed statement, while a "challenge" offers an open statement, something that can be overcome. This simple linguistic change allows the brain to start to actively look for solutions.

Take this example, looking at the problem and challenge mindsets for a scenario where someone says, "Hey, Rachel, I need you to do a workout every single day this week."

Problem Mindset

I don't have time to work out.

I don't have any workout equipment.

I don't have access to a gym or a gym membership.

I don't know how to work out properly.

Challenge Mindset

Can I get up 30 minutes earlier to work out?

What kinds of exercise do I enjoy?

What workouts can I do without any equipment?

What workouts can I do in the limited space of my bedroom or living room?

Where can I find free workout routines?

While the problem mindset only points out obstacles and leads to dead ends, the challenge mindset offers open-ended questions and different ways to think about solutions. I could easily brainstorm some solutions based on the challenge mindset questions. Maybe I can't get up early this week, but I can work out instead of watching an hour of TV after dinner. I can hit up YouTube to see what kinds of yoga or HIIT routines might be available because those types of workouts don't take much space. It's totally doable!

BE–DO–HAVE

I still remember the day I heard Terry Crews as a guest on Tim Ferriss's podcast. Terry is an excellent comedian, but in this interview, he was more serious and talked about his tough upbringing and how he wanted to be successful. To achieve this, Terry decided to take on the Be–Do–Have model, an age-old formula for achieving success that has been written about by famous figures from Stephen Covey to Ram Dass.

This model really helped me because I'd always wondered why I didn't have the things I wanted even though I was doing all the work and being friendly and professional. But I had it backward—it's not Have–Do–Be; it's Be–Do–Have. What I didn't realize was that to transform my entire life and step into my vision and business mindset fully, I first needed to imagine who I wanted to be. Most people focus on the outcome or what they want to have, but this model instead teaches to begin with who you are. Here's how it works.

1. Who Do I Want to Be?

Imagine the person you want to be and the life you want to have in full detail. It can help to think about the people who inspire you. Think about how they walk, talk, think, and act. How do they present themselves to the world and how are they perceived because of that? It helps me to write it all down.

2. What Do I Need to Do?

Once you have a clear image of the person you want to be, you will be able to see a clear path to getting there. What would that person do? You can do it too—right now!

3. What Do I Want to Have?

Write down everything that you want, everything you've been dreaming of. It might be material things such as a house or a measure of success like 100,000 followers. Nothing is selfish here; nothing is a silly answer.

Start with the person you want to *be* in order to *do* the things you need to do and *have* the things you want in this lifetime. You can't wait for things outside of your control to change—you have to be the person who makes the changes happen. By *being* a confident person, I start *doing* what a confident person does, then I *have* the things (such as opportunities) experienced by a confident person.

This can be a difficult mindset to cultivate, but you can practice applying it to everything. Even when I was considering writing a book, I realized that my thinking had started to reverse: *Maybe I'll write a book when I'm super successful!* Nope. I'm going to *be* a successful person, *do* what a successful person would do and write the book, and experience the joy and success in *having* written a book.

SOLIDIFY YOUR VISION AND INTENTION

When I'm trying to decide what comes next in business or life, I always visualize ideal outcomes. For example, at every crossroads I come to or with every decision I need to make, I literally close my eyes and visualize what the best version of me would do.

Imagining your best self—the version in your meditations and dreams—is a great way to make sure that everything you do comes from a clear vision. If you don't have a specific vision or a dream you are working on, you can actively work on developing one. It takes 5 to 10 seconds and is best done right when you wake up and the moment before you fall asleep. I personally just whisper quietly while my head is still on the pillow, "Give me a vision, God. Please." You don't have to speak to God specifically—you can just address it to the universe, a spirit guide, or any other force you feel connected to.

Once you have your vision, write it down. It can be simple; it doesn't need to be elegant. It's more important that it be heartfelt. Here are a few examples of vision expressed through intention.

I help thousands of women to love their bodies.

I serve business owners by speaking truth on stages.

I empower families to spend time together through time-saving tools and strategies.

Remember your vision board? Here is where it will come in handy because it already represents the feelings and experiences you want someday. In 2015 when I was searching for a business direction, these were some of the dreams I put on my vision board. In no particular order:

- Leave my 9-to-5
- Help Poul leave his 9-to-5
- Make $100,000
- Make $1,000,000
- Get 10 clients
- Go viral
- Get featured in big PR
- Become a *Huffington Post* contributor
- Help a client make $1,000,000

- Grow a community to 1,000 people
- Write a book
- Become a *New York Times* best-selling author
- Give a TEDx Talk
- Serve 100 students
- Get on a big podcast (ideally one of the ones I listen to!)

I realized I had absolutely no clue how to make any of these things happen. But then I got to work. I stared at my dreams every single day before starting work, and just six months after creating this vision board, I had 10 clients and replaced my income from my 9-to-5 job. Doors started to fling open because I had identified my goals. I didn't know much, but I knew where I wanted to go.

Maybe you're like, "Rachel, I don't know if this vision stuff is for me. I just need to make $1,000 per month so my rent is covered." *That is a legit mission too.* Don't ever let anyone tell you differently. Perhaps the intention behind that vision sounds like:

My business supports my family so my partner doesn't have to work a second job.

I am able to spend time with my kids because I generate revenue from home.

I take care of my body and mind by making money in my business.

The Seasons of Business

When considering your vision and intention, don't worry if any of it feels selfish. Your vision will evolve, and so will you—it all depends on your season of life. That's part of nature.

For example, I live in Minnesota, where we have four very distinct weather seasons that are a part of everyday life. You see them, you experience them, you smell them. Everything changes in Minnesota with the seasons. That's part of why I love living here. But how we act in one season wouldn't be sustainable in another season. For example, in a Minnesota winter, you bundle up in a heavy parka and snow boots. You would freeze to death if you went out wearing a swimsuit or shorts and a tank top.

Business seasons also change. Some will be busier, and some will be slower. You have to know what season you're in and adjust your behavior accordingly. Not every season can be a sprint, because life is a marathon. If a sprinter were to run a marathon at their normal pace, they would end up quickly burning out. If a marathon runner were to run a sprint at their normal pace, they likely wouldn't place.

TAKEAWAYS

- *Journal:* Do some freewriting on what you want to have. Pick out the most important things and spend time writing down ideas about what you'll need to do to get them. Finally, consider who you need to be to get those things done. Then, write out your Be–Do–Have plan to refer to as needed.

- *Reflect:* Take some time with your vision board to contemplate your vision and intention. How are they different? Have they evolved since you started reading this book?

- *Do:* Find a situation this week where you can take a problem mindset and turn it into a challenge mindset. Consider how reprogramming your mindset could help you make decisions and affect a positive outcome.

CHAPTER 4

To Hustle or Not to Hustle

Business advice can often feel overwhelming. You're online and see an entrepreneur saying how important it is to create 100 pieces of content per day. Another tells you how they work morning, noon, and night—it's the only way to get everything done. And then you see a marketer posting about only hiring top-shelf talent.

Do these methods work? They can. And when all we see are the amazing and inspirational results (and not any of the sleepless nights, big price tags, and huge teams of people accomplishing it all), it can be easy to get caught up in thinking that this extreme hustle is the only way to see results.

WHAT IS HUSTLE, ANYWAY?

First it's important to note that there's a difference between hard work and hustle. The former is fulfilling your end of a commitment to abundance, growth, and success. Hard work is direct and pre-determined action that moves you toward a specific goal. But hustle is unfocused (though still hard) work. It's kind of like throwing spaghetti at the wall and hoping that a noodle or meatball sticks.

Hustle culture is the embodiment of fear—it's fear-driven business building instead of business building from a place of abundance. It's the belief that everything you've built could disappear at any point—that if you don't work incessantly, someone will take it away from you. Building a business should be about the journey of discovering what you have to offer is worthy; meanwhile, hustle is basically feeding into all the lies that you'll never be worthy.

I recognize this mindset in myself sometimes, even to this day. Once in a while, I have this panicky moment where I will say to my team or Poul, "I need to create 100 TikTok videos today." I'm not exaggerating at all. Unsurprisingly, they'll look at me and go, "Do you really need to do that?" And that's when I'll realize this need to create is stemming from all the terrible "what if?" scenarios that pop into my head for no good reason. *If I don't post more, I'll fall behind in my business, I'll lose followers, I'll lose clients, my business will decline.* This isn't true, of course, but it's an example of how the need to hustle comes from fear, not a place of abundance, expansion, or positive movement.

I adamantly believe that hustle culture and methods like the 100-hour work week (yes, that's a thing) prevent more women, mothers, and multi-passionate humans from creating businesses. For most people, these methods do not reflect the reality of being a real human who is attempting to grow a business—especially when you're just starting out.

- What happens when you don't have a content creation team to help you create 100 pieces of content per day?

- What happens when you don't have 10 hours a day to grind your face off?

- What if your credit sucks and you didn't attend an Ivy League school to create a network of deep pockets?

- And what you don't have the funds to hire top-shelf talent? (Besides, what is top-shelf talent, anyway? What about all the other equally talented people who perhaps haven't been in the business for as long?)

Not feeling as though you measure up can be discouraging, especially when there's so much toxic positivity in the messaging about hustling. To me, it sounds kind of like this:

"Hustle your #%$@ing face off! Hustle until grind juice is dripping out of your pores! If you want your family to be happy, you'll hustle twenty-three hours a day! Hustle until you drop dead from exhaustion—I died from exhaustion three times before I was your age!"

Um, no, thanks—I work hard, but I'm not interested in anything to do with grind juice. Ew. Besides reminding us of gross things, hustle can also have a negative impact on our mental and physical health. In fact, there are so many bad side effects of overdoing it on hustle.

How about exhaustion, even if it's to the point of hospitalization?

How about damaged marriages and relationships?

How about people abandoning their family at the expense of building a business?

How about shame, guilt, a feeling that you're never doing enough?

How about burnout?

The only real season of business where I ever recommend a little bit of hustle is when you're just starting out. If you're still working a 9-to-5 on top of freelancing or don't have any income coming in, you might be working longer hours. But always make sure to leave time for yourself and the people in your life—even just a half hour where you can catch up at the dinner table or spend time reading in bed.

Advice is just advice—you don't have to take anyone's, especially if it doesn't align with your values or lifestyle needs. Remember: your definition of success is yours alone, and it doesn't have to align with anyone else's vision. Personally, I don't want the version of success that requires skipping sleep, because being well-rested is a form of success that helps me reach for my next goal.

EIGHT TIPS TO TRADE HUSTLE FOR HARD WORK

If you're looking to avoid hustle in favor of hard work, these are my recommended strategies to stay focused and not get overwhelmed.

1. Break Things Down into Manageable Tasks

One day, Poul asked me, "What are you doing today?" And I looked at my to-do list, counted 431 things, and said, "Everything, I guess." This mentality kept me from making major progress.

I didn't realize it at the time, but little steps and countdowns—breaking your day down into manageable tasks—can change your entire life. Sometimes we're so intimidated by the big, hairy, audacious goals that we do nothing. Breaking your day down into manageable tasks can change your entire life—and we'll talk about this more in Chapter 17.

One strategy that helped me came from *Unbreakable Kimmy Schmidt*, of all places. If you're not familiar, this is a Netflix show where Kimmy and three other women were held captive in a bunker for over a decade before escaping. It sounds kind of dark, but it's actually a comedy that follows Kimmy as she makes her way through the world outside the bunker. She is tirelessly optimistic, and at one point, she says something very wise: "I learned a long time ago that a person can stand just about anything for 10 seconds. Then you just start on a new 10 seconds. All you've got to do is take it 10 seconds at a time."

I couldn't get this out of my mind, and I started applying Kimmy's strategy to everything I did. And it worked! It kept me moving forward. If I had to send out cold pitches to potential clients, I would do it in batches of 10. Just 10, and then I'd take a break. And then 10 again, and then 10 again, all the way until I hit 100 per day. As another example, I used to run 6 to 12 miles several times a week, but starting back up after I had my kids was really hard. So I started counting 10 seconds at a time, six times per minute. Sixty times per mile. One hundred eighty times per run. Ten seconds became a mantra for me.

I eventually adapted this idea into an approach I call the Power 10. If you have tons of things you'd like to do, just pick 10 for the day. I like to divide my 10 up this way:

- **3 dailies:** These serve your audience, usually in the form of content creation.

- **3 priorities:** These are involved with working *on* your business, not just *in* the business.

- **3 commitments:** These just simply need to get done, whether that's meetings or client deadlines.

- **1 money-generating activity:** This is whatever actively brings in money—it could be pitching companies, sending proposals, or upselling existing clients.

If you repeat the Power 10 over and over throughout your workday with different groupings of tasks, you will achieve 10, 20, 30 things per day instead of mindlessly scrolling on Facebook while supposedly "working on the business." And, as your capacity for taking action grows, your ability to perform the Power 10 will get stronger.

A principle called Parkinson's law, which we'll talk more about a bit later in the book, comes into play here. Put simply, the amount of work you're required to do adapts to the time you have available. Have you ever had 3 minutes before the baby wakes up for a nap and suddenly something that normally takes 20 minutes becomes a 3-minute task? So Parkinson's law means that in order to get something done faster or more efficiently, you must limit the amount of time it is allowed. At first, the Power 10 might take you a full day. Later, you want to try to fit *two* Power 10s into your day. And soon, on a good day, you'll be able to fit in several.

2. Embrace Productive Sprints

Even though the traditional work day is eight hours, it's estimated that the average worker only puts in two or three hours of actual work per day. Though you'll likely be doing more work than this as an entrepreneur or business owner, one way to make the most of this time is to sprint, or to carve out an amount of time to focus solely on work.

I set aside a specific time frame every day for sprinting. Yours can be before, during, or after working hours—whenever it's best for you. Lately I've been doing 7-to-9 a.m.

sprints with some of my students in The Social Clique, an educational product geared toward helping entrepreneurs grow a business. We all wake up a little earlier and get work done together in silence—it's motivating, and it works.

Your sprint can be 20 to 30 minutes, or it can be two hours. All you have to do is pick an amount of time that makes sense and commit to it every single day. Here's what I do to make sure my time is super effective:

1. Before sprinting: take two to three minutes to focus on your Power 10. I specifically love the priorities—the things that move the needle forward. I'll pick three to five things I'd like to get done. If I only get one or two done, that's okay. If I get five done, I kicked butt!

2. Give the sprint a name. Personally, I like super-cheesy '90s names that feel over the top, like the Power Hour. You can probably come up with something a little more subtle or cool.

3. Listen to music. This one is optional, but I really like frequency-based soundtracks and/or classical music. I put headphones on or crank the speakers (depending on if the kids are sleeping). Sometimes I'll blast '80s rock. It depends on what I need to keep me focused.

4. Consider sprinting as absolutely sacred. Notifications are turned off, social media apps are closed, and it's 100 percent productivity. If you can't ignore it, put your phone in another room.

5. After sprinting: take a minute to close your eyes and ask yourself how you feel.

These sprints are amazing, and the amount of work you will accomplish over time is impressive. There's a quote from Bill Gates that I live by: "Most people overestimate what they can do in one year and underestimate what they can do in ten years." Sprints are one way to make sure you're taking consistent steps to build your ideal future.

3. Find Deadline Flexibility Where You Can

Meeting deadlines is important—it shows that you care about your commitments, it is a factor of what you're able to charge, and it can be a component of client loyalty. But when you don't hit a deadline, give yourself a little bit of grace. We're all human, and we all miss deadlines from time to time.

Sometimes deadlines are made up or scheduled early on purpose to build in extra time for delays. The key to deadline flexibility is communication—the earlier the better. If you know you're going to need more time, don't wait until the day before it's due to let others know. In addition, having a hierarchy for deadlines helps. I don't miss client deadlines for deliverables, but some of my self-imposed deadlines can be shifted around if necessary.

In addition, sometimes you'll be busier than others; for example, when I am coming out of a busy season, I'll purposely take on less to give myself a bit of a break. So, sometimes less is more. Plus, the more you practice, the more you'll be able to take on. And the better the quality of your work, the more clients will spread the word about you or come back.

4. Remember That It's Not a Competition

As with everything in life, from fitness journeys to relationships, it's easy to compare our business with others.

Society programs us to believe that while you might be doing okay, somebody else is doing better, and that means you're not good enough. This couldn't be less true.

There's so much pressure to hustle, grow faster, get awards and achievements, and prove ourselves by never slowing down. So much in our fast-paced world and culture trains us to believe that if you don't keep up, someone else is going to beat you to your goals. Yet so many of us go into entrepreneurship to *get away from* the whole idea of climbing some corporate ladder. We go into this because we're like, *I want to build something different that supports me and my life.* So I have to remember it's not about comparison. I know I need to look at the lives of other people and say, *Is what they have really what I want?*

5. Pace Yourself

Especially when you're just starting out and saying yes to everything, be wary of overcommitting. I can't take on as many clients as I would like at any given time and still deliver a high level of service to them all—it's simply not possible. So, as tempting as it is to do everything and to do it *right now*, you'll actually get more done if you'll commit to a consistent pace.

Treat your work like it's a marathon—if you're sprinting all the time, it's a surefire recipe for absolute burnout. Though goals are important, make sure they are reasonable goals that make room for you to spend time outside work. Have you ever said something like, "Just a decade before I hit my goal, so I'm working overtime," or "If I work two jobs for the next five years, I'll be able to pay my house off in cash"? If this is you, more balance is needed. Keep in mind that not every business season can be a sprint, and that there are other things in life that are worth spending time on.

6. Be Aware of the Highlight Reel

I wish I had known that most people are only showing you their highlight reel. When you look around at people on Instagram, TikTok, or YouTube, what you're seeing is a carefully crafted and curated selection of their life. They're generally not showing the blood, sweat, tears, pain, heartbreak, or days when they're literally sitting in their closet crying because they're worried about whether things will work out or fall apart. The truth is, nobody's life can be fully represented by the highlight reel, so don't waste time comparing yourself with one.

Now, there are some people who do take people behind the scenes. I try my best to take people behind the scenes, especially on my Instagram. If you look for it, you can see some of the things that are not so glamorous about being a mom of three and running several businesses. For example, I even filmed a video that literally showed off my postpartum "mom stomach." It wasn't what you'd typically see on social media or in any advertisement: no flat abs, no six-pack, just a stomach soft as crushed velvet, hiding a core strong enough to lift heavy furniture and give piggyback rides. That unfiltered image is the picture you see on the cover of this book.

7. You Are More Than Your Business

We're trained not to miss any opportunities, even when there's so much else going on. There's this idea that you have to do it all—that you have to constantly be doing more. I realized that I was often doing things because I didn't believe that I was worthy enough to be a business owner or to call myself an expert in marketing.

I started examining what my life looked like outside of courses, coaching, clients, revenue, and income, and asked myself some hard questions. What if all of that were gone tomorrow? Would I be happy with who I was? Would I be happy with how I treated my family or the friendships I built? Would I be okay if no one ever called me the Queen of Social Media again? Is who I am enough?

One day, everything just clicked. I realized I didn't have to do anything to be worthy of love and acceptance, and my business didn't define who I was. Sure, it's definitely a part of me and I'm proud of it, but it isn't everything. There is a lot more that I live for, and that reminds me it's okay to stop and say, *I don't have to do anything else today—I've kept up with my commitments and checked off my list of priorities. I can stop working.* You don't have to constantly be doing something, and there's no one you need to keep up with. It's not a race.

8. Keep Track of Changing Seasons

Your business needs, priorities, desires, and things to avoid are going to change from season to season. Perhaps the end-of-year holidays are your busiest time because everyone is buying your product as a gift. Perhaps it's the summer months when you see an influx of customers because people are taking vacations and have more time to try out your service. Or maybe you go through a season when things have to slow down because there are so many activities going on for your family. Every business is different, but the important thing to remember is that seasons are temporary. Sometimes people ask me, "Rachel, you've been working really hard the past couple of months. Are you ever going to get a break?" I will, eventually. But sometimes I'm working so hard because it's a busy season.

And so you have to continually check in and ask yourself, *What season am I in?* In practice, that means that during a busy season, you shouldn't judge yourself harshly or hold yourself to the same standards of a nonbusy season. You wouldn't go out in a snowstorm wearing shorts and say, "Why am I so cold?" Once your business settles into a consistent flow, you'll be able to see these seasons ebbing and waning, and it will be easier to plan ahead for your busy times.

TAKEAWAYS

- *Journal:* What does "hustle" mean to you? What are its positive and negative attributes? How do you differentiate hard work and hustle, and how can you avoid a hustle culture mentality?

- *Reflect:* What do the seasons of your business look like? When might you be busiest? What sort of strategies might you try to maintain a marathon pace even during the busiest times?

- *Do:* Try out one of the eight tips from this chapter, such as the Power 10 or sprinting, and keep track of how much you get done.

CHAPTER 5

Pockets of Possibility

So many small businesses fail within their first five years—nearly half! Come hell or high water, I was going to beat the odds, and when I was starting out, I desperately googled everything from "What do successful businesses have in common?" to "What are the morning routines of millionaires?" and even "Do I have to wear a blazer to be successful?"

I found a ton of advice, from the glaringly obvious (do the work!) to the absolutely bizarre (micro-dosing on LSD will help you find your best ideas). But one thing really stood out to me: it seemed as though all the advice was written by 42-year-old men who don't spend time taking care of kids.

"Beat the sunset, all legends grind at 5 a.m." Dude, the kids didn't fall asleep until 9, even 10ish. The only time I get to myself is after they're asleep, and I need eight hours of sleep to function.

"Feed your body like a million-dollar racehorse at all times, no exceptions." As if I have time to make another meal instead of chowing down on my kiddos' leftover mac-n-cheese with peas and carrots.

"Create a morning routine that includes 60 minutes of exercise, 60 minutes of meditation, reading, priming, making a green smoothie, and running to the farmer's market to pick out your herbs for the day." Um, okay, so I am lucky to get a shower in before I have to start working.

"Walk on the bare earth every morning with bare feet, connecting with the ground."

I live in Minnesota. Have you ever been barefoot in sub-zero weather?

"Invest heavily into marketing if you want to grow."

Okay, I have about $60, is that enough?

And then there was the world of toxic positivity, much of it coming from women in business. I am pretty darn positive—by choice and training, not by nature—but the advice from so many mompreneurs was also so frustrating.

"If you're not where you want to be, you're the only one to blame."

"Hide your mess and show up a success."

"Depression, anxiety, and bad days only exist because you still allow them."

"We're in America—if you're not a success, you're slacking on your dreams."

All these messages are rooted in guilt and shame, and they neglect the fact that people not only grow up with different experiences but that many are also dealing with inequities on a systemic level that they can't just ignore or easily escape.

MY STRUGGLE WITH DEPRESSION

Though outwardly I'm positive, bubbly, and put-together, I've dealt with depression and anxiety since I was 11 years old. I remember sitting in the chapel of my private school—I was a scholarship student—with my amazing teacher, Mrs. Cox. She had so much empathy for my struggle and talked to my parents about what was going on. But no one was really equipped to handle discussing mental health concerns. Back then, if you admitted that you were depressed, you were seen as crazy. In fact, depression ran in my family, but no one ever really talked about it.

I lived with depression for years. It was an all-encompassing fog that never went away. Any time I experienced relief and happiness, it would be gone as fast as I experienced it. There was always this nagging feeling inside me that something was just wrong, something was going to fall apart. Like many people, I attempted to numb my depression with alcohol. When I was about 18 years old, I started drinking to excess quite a bit. Now, in certain areas of my life, I'm an all-or-nothing person. For example, instead of eating a couple of chocolate-covered raisins, I'll eat an entire bin from Costco.

With alcohol, it was the same thing, only way more destructive. The second that it touched my lips, I was like, *I love this. It clears off the fog. It gets me out of my head. It frees me up to have fun.* And so I would keep drinking until I blacked out.

Things escalated to the point where I started drinking every single night. My family was understandably concerned. And when I married Poul, my drinking started becoming very secretive. I would put a bottle of whiskey in the closet so I could sneak swigs of it and then go back to whatever I was doing. I was drinking morning, noon, and night—even at work—and it started affecting my career. Finally, I reached my breaking point: I went to work one day and decided not to drink. On that day, my hands started shaking, and I started feeling incredibly sick. I literally felt like I was going to die; it was so scary. But I didn't drink.

That day certainly wasn't easy. In fact, the first few days, weeks, and even months after this were very challenging. All I wanted to do was drink. But it got a little easier over the following months, then years. Poul was very patient and kind. He would say, "I love you no matter what," and his support removed the shame from drinking and depression. I discovered that I was a lot stronger than I realized. I have never touched another drop of alcohol. Today, I have no desire to drink.

Getting sober was one of the best things that ever happened to me. And it's just one of many things that has kept me alive. I became a mom quite young, and, though difficult, it gave my life meaning, as did support from my dad in crucial moments when I felt as though I couldn't go on. As I got older, I also learned healthy coping mechanisms to manage living with depression. For example, I don't sleep in, because that is one of my depression triggers. Exercise is helpful for me, such as taking a brisk walk on the treadmill. Journaling with no judgment has been very beneficial, as has drinking lots of water.

These things aren't a cure for depression. For me, it's still a matter of managing and coping, and there are good days and bad days. There are still times when I've felt like staying in bed for a week. I want to do everything successful people recommend, but I'm just not up for it. Depression doesn't run my life, but it's never gone away. I used to consider depression an unexpected, unwelcome visitor. But once I started to be okay with the feeling of being sad, depression didn't feel the need to show up as much. But the lingering side effects are sometimes surprising; I often find that I can empathize with other people and their anxieties a lot better.

Whether you also have depression or are facing some other kind of struggle, you're not broken. Challenges are a part of life, and with a support system—such as family or friends—and strategies to help you keep your challenge at bay, you can be successful.

FINDING POCKETS OF POSSIBILITY

A full business cannot be built in a single hour. But I do believe it's possible to start a successful business with just one hour per day. Sometimes all we get are little pockets of possibility. What's a pocket of possibility? A small window of time where we can work with intention to build our vision. Through these pockets of possibility, we can learn new skills, connect with others, and build our business.

Notice I'm not telling you to dedicate hours a day or ignore your family. I'm not telling you to spend thousands or take out a loan for hundreds of thousands of dollars, and I'm definitely not telling you to risk your family's house or ability to eat. I'm asking you to trust in your "aha!" moments and look for opportunities throughout your day to get things done.

If it weren't for pockets of possibility, I don't know that I would have been able to get my business off the ground. I started by doing what I knew how to do in any spare moment I had. I worked in the morning before the kids were awake, during nap times, and before bed when the house was quiet. I worked over my lunch hour calling potential clients as I snuck in bites of food. It's all about finding small and manageable tasks that you can fit into these pockets of possibility. Let me break down what pockets of possibility could look like in 5-, 10-, and 30-minute increments:

5-Minute Tasks

- Proofread e-mails.
- Send the drafts in your e-mail.
- Send or answer LinkedIn messages.
- Follow up with an old lead.
- Install your Facebook pixel.
- Clean your desk.
- Clean your whiteboard.
- Update your e-mail signature.
- Refine descriptions of your products or services.
- Organize the files on your computer desktop.
- Organize screenshots on your phone.
- Rep a friend in a group.

10-Minute Tasks

- Record a video for marketing.
- Write out a standard operating procedure (SOP).
- Answer five e-mails.
- E-mail your list.
- Document a strategy.
- Pitch a prospect.
- Engage with 10 dream clients on social media.
- Create an asset.
- Create a graphic in Canva.

30-Minute Tasks

- Walk on the treadmill.
- Meditate and journal.
- Record a podcast.
- Record a YouTube video.
- Write 500 words for a blog or future book.
- Send upsell opportunities to all of your current clients.
- Create a special bundle for the next holiday.
- Leave encouraging comments on the content of 30 dream collaborators.
- Watch a YouTube video to learn a new skill set.
- Go live on social media.
- Deep clean your office.
- Create a case study.

If you're looking at your life and saying, *I don't know how I'm going to fit in everything on my to-do list,* don't panic. Change your mindset and think, *Okay, I get 20 minutes a day by myself in the car. But what if those 20 minutes are spent on client phone calls instead?* If you get a one-hour lunch break at your day job, fantastic. That gives you 20 minutes to prospect, 20 minutes to respond to e-mails, and 20 minutes to work on your marketing.

The truth is, if you wait for life to make it easy, it's never going to happen. If you say you're going to start when you have enough money or time for it to be convenient, you'll be waiting forever. You have to carve out time—or rather, find the pockets of possibility—and act on it. Because sometimes that's all we get.

TAKEAWAYS

- *Journal:* Take some time to write about the challenges that you have faced or are facing in your day-to-day life. What kind of healthy coping mechanisms have helped you? Who can you turn to when you need support?

- *Reflect:* What kinds of business advice have you heard and tried? Think about the different categories of advice and who they are coming from. Do those people's lifestyles and ideals match yours? What kind of advice do you want to take and what kind do you want to leave behind?

- *Do:* Make a list of what you need to get done and break those tasks down into 5-, 10-, and 30-minute increments. When you find your pockets of possibility, whip out your list and start crossing off items.

CHAPTER 6

Taking That Leap of Faith

The day I replaced Poul's income from his 9-to-5—meaning he could quit his job and come work with me—I had an absolute, utter breakdown. I actually drove to his work and told him, "You need to tell them that you didn't mean to quit. Tell them it was just a joke. You need to tell them you changed your mind! We can't do this." Maybe it was the feeling of the last safety net being pulled out from underneath us, but the pressure of suddenly being in charge of generating all the revenue for our family was terrifying.

I had good reason for being scared. Early on in my business journey, I learned that even things that seem solid are never guaranteed. In 2016, the week after I left my full-time job, I immediately lost close to almost $2,000 a month in income. My biggest client canceled our contract nine months early over a misunderstanding around the results of Facebook advertising campaigns. I kept this failure private, which was difficult since I was in an online community where people were constantly praising me for getting clients. In reality, I was googling "How do I find clients?" and "How do I replace clients?" I had lost thousands of dollars of income, and I didn't know how I could show my face and act confident when I was scared and so beyond stressed.

My world started spinning out of control. Fear was no longer in the background; it was driving the car. Doubt, meanwhile, had called shotgun. I also kept crying and freaking out and calling Poul while he was at work. He was my only lifeline, and I felt alone and so isolated. We didn't have a safety net in place. We had no money in savings—I mean not a single dollar—and there were very few backup plans. My social media business had to work.

When you take a leap of faith such as quitting a job with a steady income, you're naturally going to be afraid. You can be paralyzed by a swarm of "what-ifs": what if I lose all my clients, what if I can't find affordable health care, what if, what if, what if . . . Those concerns are all valid. Our leap of faith looked a lot like the Disney film *Aladdin*, when Aladdin holds out his hand to Jasmine and says, "Do you trust me?" I have had many of those conversations with Poul, where I say, "Do you trust me?" And he puts his hand in mind and I say, "Then juuuuuump!"

Since you can't control everything, it helps if you can have certainty about some things. Set yourself a goal that will let you know you're ready to jump. For example, it might be something like, "I will quit my job when I've got my first three clients lined up."

It's okay to be afraid, but don't let that fear control you. After you jump, you're probably going to hit some debris on the way down and run into issues. Lean on whatever support system you have—I would be lost without Poul. But even if you're on your own, there are some strategies you can try to keep yourself focused on your vision.

START JOURNALING

I've kept a journal since I was 11, so my poor journals have seen everything from a couple of lines of frantic emotion to five pages of venting. For me, journaling is a safe place where I share what I'm excited about as well as what feels out of alignment or is frustrating. It's a place where I go to process my emotions.

I love my therapist, and she's fantastic. But even she has opinions and feedback about the things that I share. Sometimes, it's healthy to privately vent without opinions, feedback, or judgment.

I hear you asking, "But what do I write about, Rachel?" Of course you can journal about your goals. (And, of course, throughout this book I've been giving you suggestions to journal at the end of each chapter about the topics we've covered.) But you should also capture your early thoughts—the excitement, challenges, hopes, dreams, doubts, everything. Your entries can be related to your business or your life. It's your space to let everything that's swirling around in your head out in the open. When fear and doubt kick in, your journal is your best friend. Pull it out and share everything with it, so that you don't feel like you're just bogging everyone else down with your concerns and challenges, because that will happen. When things go right, also share them in your journal. If you're ever worried about being too braggy, your journal doesn't care. It's also fascinating to look back on down the road. Journal everything. Write it all down.

Sometimes just the act of writing how I'm feeling, whether or not it's rational and warranted, is the best first step in starting to identify solutions or where I can make adjustments. Just getting it out helps you start to create order. And it's never too late to start journaling. If you're 70, you have years of experience, wisdom, regrets, and advice to write about. If you're 50, you have half your life to document, process, share, and track your growth. If you're 30 or younger, you have decades to log your life!

Tips for Journaling

1. Start by trying to write just a couple of sentences each morning. Sometimes it's one line and sometimes it becomes two pages.

2. You don't have to catch up on days or events that you miss.

3. It's not a formal essay. Just share how you feel, what's happening, or any random thoughts on your brain.

4. Be honest and don't hold back. No one is going to publish your journal!

5. Though I recommend journaling every day, don't beat yourself up for missing a day (or a month!).

Each journal you have can be a representation of a certain chapter of your life. When I become a new person in my business and how I lead, I start a brand-new journal to represent that change. Best of all, you can start journaling right now, no experience required. Your journal is a noncommittal, judgment-free zone for everything that you're feeling.

FIND WAYS TO PIVOT

Right after I left my 9-to-5 job and lost my major anchor client, I did what any rational human would do—I bawled my face off. And then I wrote a children's book, page by page, on white printer paper.

I wrote a book that spoke to the sad, scared, lost, lonely, confused, and doubting little girl inside me. I thought, *You know what, I'm going to write a book while I'm crying. I'm going to write a book that some kids can read, so that they never doubt themselves again.* This was my way of expressing the part of me that felt rejected, frustrated, and like I was letting everyone down. I hung the pages across the dining room walls. When my mind wandered to the impending failures I figured were coming, I glanced at the pages. Seeing the story I wrote would instantly give me life, and it kept me going for several reasons.

As a kid, I wanted to be an author more than anything, but I put that dream aside for many years, trying to convince myself that it was too big or unrealistic. But then, at a very dark moment when I was at my worst, I made that dream become reality. It wasn't so much that I was thinking, *Well, since I failed at that, I'll have a go at this other dream.* It was more that I was falling back on something that comforted me—writing—in my time of need.

I also saw that I was capable of accomplishing things and that I did have an important message to offer the world. Those pages represented more than the story—they represented my dream. Dreams are a natural extension of who we are. Big, small, unrealistic, grandiose—all these dreams matter. Sometimes your dreams will be absolutely demolished or you'll realize you need to find new dreams, but that's part of the process. You can learn valuable lessons about how to pivot and refocus your efforts. In fact, sometimes the best lessons in life come right after a big failure. Once the feelings of sadness and rejection fade away, you learn what's important. You'll figure out new dreams eventually, even if it takes a while.

After all, your dreams aren't accidents. They're always there, trying to help you become the person that you need to be in this lifetime. Our dreams matter—because we matter.

TAKEAWAYS

- *Journal:* Are there any "what-ifs" that are currently knocking at your door? Get them out on the page. You don't have to come up with solutions now, but just acknowledging what you're afraid of is a start.

- *Reflect:* Are you ready to take a leap of faith? Think about the ways you are poised to succeed. If you don't feel ready, what do you need to get there?

- *Do:* Perhaps you've just been jotting down some notes here and there as you read this book, but now is the moment to get yourself a real journal and start writing! Document successes and failures, dreams, even just that breakfast you made that was so spectacular. Try journaling for 20 minutes every day this week and just see what happens.

Part II

PRESENCE

CHAPTER 7

Marketing versus Social Media Strategy

On February 4, 2016, I typed out and posted a short and sweet Facebook post:

Yes, I know that my wedding ring is small.

> *Friends and family often ask me when I'm going to have it "upgraded."*

> *After all, it doesn't represent the level of success we are achieving.*

> *I've even had one person say, "You could wear a bigger diamond for important events, so people don't think you're not successful."*

> *Wait a minute: Since when did the size of someone's ring become an indication of success?!*

> *For me, the ring is SO much more.*

My ring symbolizes a whirlwind, storybook, "make you sick" love story. It reminds me of how my husband and I met and fell in love in one night at a Perkins diner.

He worked as a window washer, and I was a single mother.

One short week later, and we professed our love to one another, him leading the conversation.

We couldn't stop dreaming of our future, so excited to have a baby, buy a house, and fall asleep together every night.

We couldn't wait for the future. So we didn't.

Thirteen days after meeting, we eloped. I didn't even think about a ring until my husband surprised me before the ceremony. He drained his savings to gift me with a small token of his love.

I say small only because it pales in comparison with how big his love is, even now, after years of marriage.

That, my friends, is success to me.

I included a picture of my left hand, wearing my 0.25-carat pavé-cut diamond ring, alongside those words. My nails are painted a shiny, cherry-red color, and if you looked closely, you can see my slightly torn cuticles, a tangible sign of anxiety-filled days of the not-so-distant past.

The photo's backdrop was an old Boppy pillow my daughter relied on when she was a baby. After she outgrew it, I used it to prop up my laptop as I worked on the couch after the kids went to bed.

I didn't expect anything to come from this post. I was working my side hustle from 7 p.m. to 2 a.m. in addition to my 9-to-5 job. I was exhausted and just letting off a little steam, trying to keep in focus the things that were most important in my life. But a few months later in April, the magic hit full force, and what I wrote started picking up traction. The post had reached 60,000 people when, one morning, I woke up to thousands of notifications on my phone. I opened Facebook to see what the heck was going on—and the post's numbers kept creeping up even more.

300,000 reached . . .

3,000,000 reached . . .

5,000,000 reached . . .

When all was said and done, in a week, the post reached *11.3 million people*, gained 300,000+ reactions and 50,000+ shares.

I went viral!

Cosmopolitan, Daily Mail, Huffington Post, Glamour, and dozens more online magazines and public relations sites— they all shared my silly little post. Then, NBC's *Today* show called me. I literally thought I was being pranked by a family member or friend—but, no, they really wanted to feature me. And I got a tweet from Sealy, which wanted to send us a brand-new mattress—a truly generous and welcome gift as I was sleeping on a 20-year-old mattress with stains and broken springs.

(P.S.: Thank you, Sealy. That was one of the kindest things anyone has done for me—and I plan on repaying you someday, somehow.)

I started feeling bold and decided to track down Arianna Huffington's personal e-mail address. I reached out and asked to become a contributor to *The Huffington Post*. Arianna replied and said yes. And then I pitched a big podcast, *Entrepreneurs on Fire with John Lee Dumas*. They said yes too!

SOCIAL MEDIA STRATEGIES

It was sheer luck my post took off like it did—social media is unpredictable. The kinds of posts that are popular on one platform fall flat on another. Changes to algorithms mean your posts are no longer seen by a broad audience without a paid boost. In addition, the kinds of content people want to see often change from week to week as trends fall into (and out of) fashion. During stressful times, users might be more interested in lighthearted posts rather than anything too emotionally heavy. Sometimes the posts that get eyeballs don't always create sales or convert customers. Above all, the design and functionality of every social media platform changes constantly and sometimes drastically—often without warning. I recall one memorable time when I was preparing to give a talk in which I referenced a feature of a certain platform. An hour before I was due onstage, I searched for the latest changes. I was glad I did—the platform had changed, and I needed to make some last-minute edits to my talk!

Such uncertainty is the reason why I'm going to discuss certain social media strategies rather than certain social media platforms in this section. Many of the strategies related to social media can be completely evergreen. I heard this quote from someone years ago, and it's stuck with me: "If you know the process, the platform doesn't matter."

Be the Producer, Not the Consumer

Most people have social media because it's fun. It's a way to connect with friends or even celebrities. You can find out what's going in the world and learn just about anything. But mostly, you probably spend time viewing social media as a consumer instead of as a producer. In other words, you're often so busy enjoying content, you're not necessarily thinking about marketing.

I highly recommend spending time on social media— but spend your time wisely. It's far too easy to default to browsing instead of detecting and analyzing patterns, so be sure to focus your time. Remember when we talked about research (see Chapter 2)? Practice getting into a research mindset every time you open one of these apps by collecting screenshots and taking notes. Then, you can apply what you learned to your own strategies.

Don't Be Afraid to Try New Platforms

Spending time online is certainly great preparation for a social media career. I'm proof of that: I started working in social media completely by accident, in no small part because I'm a digital native.

Like many kids of a certain age, I started off as a member of Neopets, an online platform where you take care of virtual pets (if you know, you know!). Later I graduated to MySpace, which I loved—I even learned how to code so I could make my page look really cool—and then switched to Facebook. From there, I joined Instagram, Twitter, LinkedIn, TikTok—if it was available, I had an account.

I remember tweeting at the reality stars from shows such as *Keeping Up With the Kardashians* or *The Bachelor*. Sometimes they would tweet back, and I would feel a flare of excitement. That feeling was my first indication that, wow, this is fun, and it's something I could actually do. Though I put that inkling of a dream on the back burner while I tried a few different careers, I started using social media again when I became a hairstylist. I couldn't really afford anything to promote myself, but social media was free. I studied what celebrities were doing and noticed they all showed up with this unapologetic confidence. I thought,

What if I just started doing that for my hair business? I started showcasing pictures and videos of big color transformations, extensions, and prom updos. And it worked! I just kept posting on social media—and the more I posted, the more people seemed to find me and hire me.

Marketing Is Not the Same as Social Media

Marketing and social media go hand in hand. They inform each other, like a Venn diagram where most of social media overlaps with marketing. Your marketing skills (like public relations) are transferable to social media channels. In fact, social media is a great place to test marketing theories. If you want to try out a certain tagline, customer pitch, or offer, you can put it on social media and see how it performs before adopting it more widely.

Though the aim of marketing and social media is the same—to get clients or customers to buy what you're offering—marketing and social media *strategies* aren't one and the same. Marketing strategies are specifically related to things such as media outreach and communications. Social media strategies involve creating and pushing out content or messages on social media platforms.

As a result, social media strategies are often more tailored to an individual platform. In other words, they need to be adapted before they can be used for marketing. However, a marketing strategy just needs light adaptations before it can be used on social media. All this will become crucial when you start setting up your social media presence.

TAKEAWAYS

- *Journal:* Consider the differences between your marketing strategies and social media strategies. Perhaps make your own Venn diagram showing how they overlap and diverge.

- *Reflect:* What makes a post go viral? Find a few of these and think about their similarities and differences. Is there anything predictable about this kind of content?

- *Do:* Get on a few different social media platforms and play around. What are the changes that you've seen in social media, both in new platforms and how older platforms function? What is useful about social media? What is challenging about it?

CHAPTER 8

Setting Up Your Social Media Presence

A few years ago, my friend Annie Grace told me about this new social media platform called TikTok. Immediately, I told myself I needed to figure out TikTok because I saw all the signs that it was like other successful and enduring social media platforms:

- Posts got a disproportionate amount of views.
- It started dictating culture, not just copycatting it.
- Celebrities moved to the platform.

And the biggest sign of all, and the reason I knew TikTok was going to be here to stay: the next generation (hey, Gen-Zers!) moved to and embraced the platform.

And so far, it's done just that. It's been pretty successful for me.

So, here are my tips on getting started on social media and making it work for you and your business goals.

THE GOLDEN RULES

Though there are some more specific strategies about choosing and using social media platforms that I share in this chapter, if you follow these two golden rules, you will be well on your way to success.

Pick the Platform(s) You Love

I recommend first picking the social media platform you like using—it's as simple as that! Your audience is most likely on every platform, so any of them can work. Your content is going to be better if you pick platforms that you actually enjoy being on because you're going to be more enthusiastic about creating content, doing research, and engaging with followers and potential clients.

Be Your Authentic Self Online

Being your authentic self online is so, so important. For so long, I was afraid to do this. I felt like I was hiding who I really was. That's because people will try to push your buttons on social media, especially when you have content going viral. I was afraid that if I responded and let people see I was upset, they would continue trying to push my buttons to trigger a response.

But then, a couple of years ago, I decided to start showing more of my real self online. When I started using Tik-Tok, I just started creating videos without worrying how I came across or wondering how it would affect my business. I made funny videos (or at least what I thought were funny videos) as well as educational videos. I tried everything. Most of them are still up on my page, and they're pretty cringy to watch now. But the point is that I wasn't afraid to try everything and just be myself. When things started to click and my followers started growing, it was partly because I was having fun with it and just being myself.

What's wild is that TikTok was the first time that I ever said, *I'm just going to be myself on this platform.* At first, a lot of marketers and business owners teased me for what was going on. They were like, "Oh my gosh, how's the little TikTok thing going? Can you do this dance?" I was like, "Hahahaha. I'm going to keep growing—and soon, you're going to want to hire me for it." It did happen, and I continued to grow. This is always going to be a special platform for me. I have more than 1 million followers, and by the time this book comes out, I'll be somewhere above that.

HOW TO CHOOSE YOUR PLATFORMS

Whether you're an expert or a novice on what social media platforms are available and how they work, figuring out which platforms to sign up for and then focus on for your business can be overwhelming. Every platform seems important because every channel has the potential to expand your audience. However, I recommend following these three guidelines when formulating your social media strategy.

Stick with One to Three Platforms

It can feel like a new social media platform pops up every week. That creates very real FOMO: it's easy to think that you'll miss out if you don't join each of them *right away.* However, not every platform sticks around. And, perhaps more importantly, omnipresence is a recipe for burnout—you can't be everywhere at once. In the beginning, focus on one, two, or three platforms, the ones you feel most comfortable with and have the time to nurture.

It is important to diversify your presence at some point, however. Social media can be volatile. The platform that made you famous could disappear any day. Remember Vine, the app where you made six-second videos? It was bought by Twitter and shut down—and many Vine stars disappeared overnight as well. You can't depend on one channel for everything.

Choose Long-Term Platforms

A long-term platform is one where the shelf life of content is longer. In other words, your posts won't disappear after 24 hours, as they do on Snapchat, or need to be archived manually, as on Instagram Stories. Your content is valuable, and you want to put it on platforms that don't change up as fast, such as Pinterest and YouTube, or create content that's permanent, like a podcast or blogs. All of these are considered long-term content.

For example, in 2021 I jumped on a new live audio broadcast platform called Clubhouse, where people would gather to chat. But within about a week, I deleted the platform. Why? Number one, there was no video, so it was difficult to connect with people and it felt like everyone was multitasking. Number two, the content disappeared as soon as you finished broadcasting and there was no way to access it again. And then third, the platform wasn't very searchable. All of these issues made Clubhouse an instant no for me.

Choose Searchable Platforms

Not every social media platform has robust search functionality. (Think about how many times you've had to type in multiple phrases or keywords to find the information you *actually* needed.) However, the better platforms allow people to search for and then discover content. I've found that Pinterest, YouTube, and TikTok are best in this case.

Searchable content is valuable for many reasons, such as if you're trying to address the pain points of and solve problems for clients. For example, I knew that people searching for the phrase "content plans" needed a useful solution offered by one of my current clients. By creating a video that focused on content plans, we grew my client's overall views on that one video by 300 percent as compared to others. At another point, I created videos for my own business after discovering that people were searching online for "how do I film a TikTok" or "how do I create and edit a TikTok." If you google either of those phrases, I'm in the top three search results for both.

TEXT VERSUS PHOTO VERSUS VIDEO CONTENT

There are different types of content you can share on social media platforms, all of which have pros and cons. A text-driven platform allows you to create more content a lot faster. However, on the downside, it can also feel very anonymous. It can be difficult for people to get to know you, and it's more difficult to tap into a feeling of deep connection.

Adding photos or other images won't necessarily help connect you with your audience. In my experience, photos add very little benefit as compared with text-only platforms.

I've found it's like exposing yourself with all the risk of people making fun of the way that you look.

While video content takes more time to produce and is the most vulnerable type of content, it also offers the most room for you to show your authentic self. In addition, videos are going to last longer. You get to create personalized content that truly resonates with people. And you can build a parasocial relationship with your audience—the fastest way to build, get to know, like, and trust them. A parasocial relationship essentially stimulates the part of our brain that is responsible for lighting up when we meet with a friend. When we watch someone's videos, we connect with them in a similar way.

With all this in mind, I started having all of my clients record video as the first part of their marketing strategies for social media. Our goal in this case was to reach more people and increase sales with video. The results were huge. This strategy helped one of our clients get purchases for dollars on the 1000s. Focusing on video helped another client 10x their business in a year.

At the time I am writing this book, all social media platforms are favoring video content. On the plus side, that's going to help you to grow your business significantly faster. However, tapping into the parasocial relationship isn't always comfortable for everyone. You might be shy or are wary of giving away too much personal information. At the end of the day, it's super important to know that there's no such thing as a right or wrong platform to choose. Choose the platform that feels right for you—that allows you to produce the kind of content *you* love.

Choosing Your Handles

Follow a few best practices when you're choosing your username (or handle).

1. **Have your handles be the same across all platforms.** I'm a huge fan of picking one handle to use across all of my active social media channels. It might not always be the perfect name, but changing your handle is often more difficult than it's worth. On some platforms, you can't change your name once you've chosen it. On others, you may have to wait 30 days. The major downside to changing your handle is that it might damage your brand recognition. For me, "Rachel Pedersen" wasn't available everywhere, so I added a Mrs. to my name. And that's why I'm Mrs. Pedersen on my social media channels!

- **Make sure the handle you want is available on platforms.** This goes for platforms you're using now, as well as platforms you want to expand to in the future. In fact, on the day that you pick one handle, I recommend signing up that username on all platforms, so the handle is yours when you need it. You can use the free tool Namechk.com to check availability of handles on all platforms at the same time.

2. **Keep your handle super memorable.** Make your social media name easy to spell and pronounce. You may even want to have a couple of friends look at your proposed name before you pick it to make sure there aren't any surprising (mis)interpretations you've overlooked.

TAKEAWAYS

- *Journal:* Putting yourself—your real self—out there online is scary. What makes you feel vulnerable? What makes you feel strong? How can you overcome that discomfort and make it work to your advantage?

- *Reflect:* When you are on social media, what kind of content are you attracted to? What kind of information are you seeking out? What gets you to click?

- *Do:* Make a list of the potential handles you'd like to use for your business social media accounts. Put them on a sticky note where you'll see them, and spend a few days considering them. Get the opinions of a few other people, and make sure that they are available on all the platforms you want to use.

CHAPTER 9

Connection through Content

Content is like a movie trailer for your brand. It allows people to get a sense of your overall vibe and what they can expect from you. Especially if it's a personal brand, content is the only place outside of advertisements where people can really start to know, like, and trust you.

CREATE SUCCESSFUL CONTENT

Though the specifics of successful content look different for everyone, my definition of successful content is when it resonates with your dream audience. To achieve this goal, I'm a big fan of using an authentic and personal tone. Don't try to be anyone else—be you. Write your content in a way that sounds like you speak. A good way to get started is to write a piece of sample content, then have a friend or family member evaluate it.

As I discussed in the previous chapter, I tend to prefer video content over photos and text. However, what matters more is creating content that feels like a natural extension of you, then you can test different kinds of content over time and see how you retain and grow your audience.

Here are five other ways to create successful, engaging content.

Be Consistent

Across every social media platform you use, take a consistent tone, and make it a point to schedule content on a steady basis. Give your audience a reason to visit your site consistently, and you'll stay top of mind.

Create a Brand Board

When it comes to branding, it can be helpful to have a brand board so that elements such as colors and typefaces are unified and aren't all over the place. Once you have your branding elements in place, you can access free tools such as Canva or similar sites to help you develop very professional-looking graphic designs.

Learn Best Practices

I'm a huge fan of studying other people's content—especially content from your industry or similar industries—and analyzing what's working. For copywriting especially I've found success by finding content that's performing well, writing down observations, and identifying text or tone patterns.

For example, I studied hundreds of YouTube videos and discovered that there were around 50 common ways successful videos were titled. I'm also a big fan of social monitoring—in other words, seeing what kinds of conversations people are having online and taking note of what they ask when they're not being prompted to think of a question. A great place for this is Facebook groups where entrepreneurs hang out.

Keep in mind that when you're looking at successful content, you want to model what's working—not steal it outright. It's okay to be inspired by someone else's ideas, but people shouldn't be able to look at your content and say, "Wow, this is directly modeled from that."

Read Books

You already know I'm a huge fan of reading. As I mentioned in Chapter 2, books are an amazing way to get one-on-one time with people you look up to and learn how to apply their methods to your own aims. Whether you're looking for business books, memoirs, or more technical books teaching you how to write copy, there's a wealth of resources out there to give you what you need.

Embrace Keywords

Searching for keywords is a great way to develop content leads. Get into your audience's head—what are they struggling with? For example, maybe they're googling "how to get e-mail list subscribers" or "free stock photos," or using a specific hashtag. This works both for the services or products I'm providing as well as things I'm working on for my clients.

CONNECT WITH COMMUNITY

Many times, conversations about marketing revolve around questions such as:

- What should our logo look like?
- Do we love the vibe of our website?
- Are we obsessed with our products and packaging?

These questions are centered around *you* and what *you* need and want. That might not be what your customers are looking for, however. Instead of trying to convince them that what you love is what they need to love as well, start by understanding who they are, what they need, and what their desires are. When you create content with your customers in mind first, your relationship with them is stronger. It allows you to say, "Hey, listen, we're on the same side. I'm here to help you." It helps to imagine the person you're trying to reach is someone you love very deeply, and they only have a couple moments to get the answers they so desperately need.

My marketing philosophy revolves around serving people first—it's all about who you can help. When creating content, I think, *How can I serve my people?*—not *How can I serve myself?* It's a flip from brand-first to consumer- or audience-first. You're sharing a message with the people the content is meant to serve—not crafting a message you think someone else wants to hear.

Find Content-Volume Balance

On social media, a big part of engagement and community-building is finding content-volume balance. Post too much, and people are going to get overwhelmed and maybe unfollow you. Post too little, and people won't remember or engage with you.

If you're just starting out, I recommend starting by posting once a week. This not only gives potential followers some time to learn what to expect from you, it also gives you a chance to see how much work goes into this type of content creation. Your time and energy are just as important as user experience. In general, before deciding on a content volume, I suggest doing a test to learn what kind of schedule works for you. For example, I map out three months of content. After that time is up, I evaluate what each and every day looked like: what worked, what didn't, and what makes sense moving forward.

I have several modes of content volume. Maintenance mode usually looks like one post per day, per platform. In growth mode, when I'm trying to grow my brand presence and engage more with followers, I post two to five times a day per platform. When I get into sprint mode, it might be as much as 10 or more times per day per platform. These numbers are just an example, by the way—they shouldn't be taken as a hard-and-fast rule. What works for me might not work for you.

Content volume also depends on the platform. For example, you can post a ton of short-form content and people won't get sick of it. In contrast, if you posted 10 YouTube videos in a day, you're going to absolutely burn out, and people can't absorb that much content in one day anyway.

Identify Pain, Problems, and Villains

I start everything that we create for our business with a list of pain, problems, and villains. These could all be the same—or different. Pain could be, "My marriage is struggling while I'm building this business." A problem might be, "I don't know how to hire the talent that I'm looking for." Villains could be a lawsuit that a client is experiencing.

Connect Deeply with Early Engagers

Your early engagers and commenters are super special even if they never become customers or clients. These are the enthusiastic fans who have been with you since day one, are excited to get to know you, and are going to watch as you grow and blossom. Their support can be incredibly helpful—even if just to cheer yourself up on a bad day. If you see them, hear them, and appreciate them, it will make them feel important and they'll stick around.

Create in Your Unique Voice

You will never, ever, *ever* attract your dream audience—at least not for long, and not without losing your soul—trying to be someone else. This is big, and I can't stress it enough. Create in your own unique voice, whether that's polished or rough. You're a human who is in progress, so it's more than okay to be human! Your content will grow with you. But let people feel your heart through your content—whether it's emotional or even silly. Don't try to be like the other brands; there is no way that you *have* to be.

Obviously, you want to study up on communication and copywriting skills so you're putting forth the best version of you. But when I started being myself on social media, good things happened. So much freedom came from not being afraid to be vulnerable or goofy. Best of all? It even helped my business grow. Entrepreneur Dean Graziosi and his team approached me about consulting for their business and decided to hire me. At first, I was worried, thinking, *Oh my gosh—did they see my TikTok videos?* When I met with their team, I even said, "You guys hired me despite my TikToks?" And they said, "Girl, we hired you *because* of your TikToks. You are *who you are*. And it is so great."

TAKEAWAYS

- *Journal:* Who do you see as the community you want to reach? Write about what those people want, the questions they might need answered, and anything else that comes to mind. There's no right answer—it's more about getting into the mindset of your clients or customers.

- *Reflect:* What does your unique voice sound like? When do you feel most yourself, most comfortable? How can you be more *yourself* on social media?

- *Do:* Sketch out a plan for content creation for the next month (or more!). How often do you want to post? What kind of content do you want to try (text, photos, videos)? Make a plan to create that content and get to it.

CHAPTER 10

Social Media Growth

Once you've established your social media channels, content direction, and voice, the next step is growth. In a perfect world, you could sit back, relax, and watch your carefully developed strategies pay dividends. However, reality is far more unpredictable.

BEST PRACTICES FOR GROWTH

You're always going to need to tweak your strategies and content as platforms change, your audience grows, and new trends emerge. Here are some best practices to get you started.

Create Something of Value Every Single Day

Slow and steady wins the social media growth race—which is why it's best to work your way up to creating and pushing out a piece of valuable content every single day, even if it's something small. You just never know what's going to happen or who might see the content you're putting out in the world. Opportunities surface when you least expect them.

For example, for a client in the weight-loss space, we created a post asking a question about dieting and exercise. It received *500 comments* in the first hour. Another time, we had a client reaching 200,000 people per month on Pinterest—for free!—just with steady posting. My own business has experienced multiple benefits from valuable content. I had one video reach 6 million views on TikTok. Another one that didn't go as viral reached executives at American Express, who then wanted to partner with me on training for small-business owners.

Utilize Paid Advertising—or Not!

Once you establish your social media channels, you'll probably be approached to try out some paid advertising. Experts might also recommend investing in marketing. However, do not invest money into marketing or social media advertising until you have a converting offer in place. This means that people who see your content are clicking through and completing a specific goal—it might be making a purchase or signing up for an e-mail list. Your advertising will be most effective once you've built an audience base that's already engaged with your business.

Paid advertising offers multiple pros and cons.

- Pro: You can scale very quickly.
- Con: You may not be ready to handle that level of growth.

- Pro: You learn a lot very fast.
- Con: You're paying to learn, and it can be expensive.

- Pro: You can reach new audiences.
- Con: You can reach the wrong audiences very easily.

- Pro: You can ramp up your advertising as much as you want; there's no limit.
- Con: The results might cost more than you make.

Add Calls to Action (Where Appropriate)

Growing your audience is like inviting them into your world. Once you do that, a call to action shows them where to go next; these are suggestions of what the customer can do if they want to learn more. People respond really well to action steps. You don't have to be super-promotional or apply pressure to customers—for example, you don't have to say, "Go buy my products now!" It can be simple things, like:

Join my mailing list to receive more weekly insights.
For more, go to the link in my bio.
I'm hosting a free training, and you're invited—click here.

Schedule a Weekly Social Media Check-In

Every week, set aside a dedicated time to analyze your social media results. Identify what worked and what didn't and see if you can identify any patterns. Maybe your lowest-performing posts had a negative tone, or videos received far more shares than photos. Write down several takeaways and implement any tweaks the following week.

In addition to looking at your own content, study the brands that are crushing it, your competitors, and the videos and content going viral—whatever is doing really well and receiving lots of engagement. Then, look for the words and phrases being used in this successful content. You can use a free word cloud generator—which gathers common words in a jumble that looks like an art graphic—to identify common words. When I'm studying videos, I also look for a few different clues that might give me insight into why something is performing well. Take note of what the backgrounds look like, what people are wearing, and what tone of voice they are using.

WHEN IT ISN'T WORKING

If things aren't working, the first thing to do is make a list of all the reasons why that might be. Sometimes writing things out shows you fixes you can make right away. Next, you might want to bring in fresh eyes. Getting a different perspective from someone outside your business can be super helpful when you've hit the limits of your skill set. This could be a coach or mentor, a colleague, or someone you respect. Don't ask people who are not getting results for feedback.

Having realistic expectations is key. Many of my clients initially want me to oversee their Instagram accounts but quickly realize that it's very difficult to go viral there. When you aren't seeing the results you expect on one platform, you might try to focus your attention on another.

At other times, you might think something is going wrong because you haven't had a post receive a lot of attention lately. However, perhaps you've seen increased engagement—more comments, likes, or shares—with what you have posted or you've recently increased your follower count. In many cases, success is all about a bunch of small wins, building up over time.

People also often incorrectly think that marketing and social media growth is linear. They might think that if they post X number of videos each day, they'll see Y amount of incremental growth. Usually, they overestimate how much they're going to grow in the first month or the first year. The truth is that growth happens over time. It is minimal, minimal, minimal—then it jumps sharply and things start to take off.

Don't Be Afraid to Pivot

If your social media strategy isn't working, don't be afraid to come up with a plan B, C, D, and even E. That's often necessary, in fact. One time, while I was running Facebook ad campaigns for a client, their Facebook advertising account was suddenly shut down. I was upset; we had been *crushing it*. At a moment's notice, we had to change the entire strategy so that it didn't involve buying advertising. That's not easy, especially with the way Facebook's algorithm operates. However, we built up audiences to retarget—meaning people familiar with the client to advertise to—and things ended up working out in their favor once they recovered their account because we had built an even stronger foundation and reach.

Having to start over from scratch can seem daunting. But you also might be surprised at the ways your existing skills offer unexpected advantages. For example, if you know how to set up livestreams via existing technology such as Zoom or Facebook Live, you can go to businesses and teach others how to broadcast events online. Don't undermine any of the skills you have—or take them for granted.

A few years ago, I had a conversation with a client who was looking to recruit new financial advisors. The client planned on hosting recruitment meetup events where they would teach a master class. But he was unexpectedly unable to attend the event on-site. He asked me what to do, and it was an incredible aha moment for me. I said, "Easy. Let's take this online and turn this into a virtual meetup." He thought it was awesome. Their whole team pivoted within the week, and we were even able to set it up to be an evergreen class.

Don't forget: you can be a knight in shining armor to potential and existing clients. You know how to do things they need. And when you start a business using these skills, you fill a valuable niche.

TAKEAWAYS

- *Journal:* When things aren't working out the way you hoped, it can be disheartening. Let your journal be a place where you let out all your frustration—better out than in! Once you're past your feelings, you can be fully focused on solutions.

- *Reflect:* What does valuable content look like for your business? What are other businesses in your industry creating? Look at what is successful and what isn't. How can you make your content unique?

- *Do:* Conduct an analysis of your social media strategy on a regular schedule—say, every Friday—and identify any tweaks that need to be made.

Part III

PROGRESS AND PROFIT

CHAPTER 11

Business-by-Design

In the first three years of building my business, I was working 100 hours a week, including all-nighters. I responded to clients immediately, any time they reached out. I had one client who sent me 200-plus messages in a single day, which was my fault because I responded to all of them.

I was not eating enough because I was stressed and chugging 20 cups of coffee a day just trying to stay awake. I was so sleep-deprived that I once left a comment online that I have no recollection of—I must have done it in my sleep.

Thankfully, my kids didn't suffer, but I didn't have any friends outside of business relationships. I also wasn't making my marriage a priority, and Poul and I started growing apart. The real low point came after I accepted an award for the first time our business crossed the million-dollar mark, because Poul and I got into a huge fight afterward.

I found myself breaking down almost every single day, just having these absolute meltdowns. I was falling apart because I was working too much and taking on too much—but I didn't realize that at the time. I thought the problem was me, so I tried to be more disciplined in my work, but not with my boundaries around work. I tried making myself more accessible so I could put out fires faster. I started working on weekends, nights, and anytime that my kids weren't active. In fact, one time I pulled a double all-nighter so I could clear my to-do list because it stressed me out that it was always full.

Yet when I woke up the next day after sleeping in until noon, the to-do list started ramping up again. And that's when I realized, *This is never going to be done*. It was like trying to shovel the driveway when snow is still falling. And, while my strategy was yielding success for my business, it was at the expense of my health and everything else in my life. All my relationships were strained. I was exhausted and looked sickly. I was beyond burned out.

CREATING YOUR BUSINESS-BY-DESIGN PLAN

I knew something had to change, because working at that pace wasn't sustainable. And so I came up with a solution I call business-by-design. Business-by-design is all about boundaries in a world where our priorities have to shift constantly. New clients and opportunities always come up. People tag you left and right on social media. The phone won't stop ringing. Notifications continually require our attention. A client post goes viral.

If you're caught off guard by these changes, you might feel unbalanced or overwhelmed. The same thing is true in your business *and* your life. But if you're prepared to expect the unexpected, you can weather changes more easily. As you build out your business, following a business-by-design plan can help.

Here's what makes a successful business-by-design.

Know Why You're Running the Business

First and foremost, you need to be clear on why you're even in this business. If you recall from Chapter 1, finding your why is a crucial part of starting your business. The why is often personal, so this might require soul-searching. In addition, it might change over time, so it's worth occasionally reinvestigating. For example, you could be like, *I need to make sure that my family's basic needs are paid for.* But once that happens, then you may start asking yourself, *What is the meaning of my life?* Understanding your why will drastically change the way you look at your business from day one.

Budget Your Time—and Finances—Intentionally

One of the best ways to become more efficient in your job and have a thriving business is to implement a budget with intention. But when it comes to budgets, let me just say this: getting more money is not a budgeting strategy. A lot of people thought that when my business had crossed a million dollars, we were rolling in dough, flying on jets—that our lives were all figured out. Believe it or not, budgeting is actually easier when you don't have a lot of money because your paycheck just goes to pay the bills, and that's it.

And the truth is, I was terrible at budgeting. I suddenly thought I was operating at Oprah levels of generosity. I bought my in-laws a car, invited my family to Disney World, paid for my in-laws plus my kids to go on vacation, and fixed my teeth. I was literally spending money faster than I could make it. When we were making $80,000 or $90,000 a month, I sometimes wouldn't make payroll, so I'd have to launch a product two days before payroll just to make sure we could make ends meet. This was irresponsible and privileged on my part—I see that now. But at the time I didn't know what I didn't know about finances.

Don't be like me. The sooner you can implement a budget—and have a clear budget going into each and every month—the sooner you can actually leverage your money and make it work for you. What worked for me was looking at the profit and loss (P&L) statement and making clear financial and budget decisions before spending any money.

If you don't have a budget, it's a lot like walking around the grocery store when you're hungry without a shopping list. You spend way more than is necessary and don't actually end up with the things that you need.

Make Sure Your Work/Life Divisions Are Clear

In general, it's important to put clear boundaries around your work day. Implement consistent start and end times, as well as defined office hours and turnaround time for communication.

I'm also always on some form of messaging, whether it's texting or calling or something else. You probably are too, both with friends and coworkers—and coworkers who have become friends. Figuring out the dividing line between work and life is key.

My executive assistant, Kellyanne, and I have a friendship outside of my business. So we created a clear boundary that texting and calling are for friendships or emergencies only. If one of us isn't responding over Facebook Messenger, the only time we ever start texting is if it's about one of those two categories. That's it. Otherwise, we just assume the other person is busy.

Streamline Client Communication

In my business, we take emergencies very seriously. However, "emergency" is a very strong word, and they are super rare in our business. In fact, many times what other people think are emergencies just aren't. When the occasional emergency does happen, it helps to have everything a client needs in one place. So I highly recommend that you limit your forms of client communication to one, maximum two, channels. If your clients are texting you, Facebook messaging you, Slacking and WhatsApping you, and tagging you on TikTok, that's a really good sign that you don't have enough business-by-design restrictions in place.

I recommend having general communication take place on a system or app besides your e-mail, as it's so easy for things to get lost there. Some people prefer the instant messaging on Slack; some people love the project management system Trello. You could have a dedicated drive just for your clients so that you know their content and e-mails are in one place.

Create How-We-Work Documents

Your time away from work is important—in fact, it's sacred. We implemented something that defines boundaries and brings a lot of peace of mind for our entire team: how-we-work documents. We send these documents to every client as part of our contract and onboarding process. The document outlines things such as:

- How do we communicate with you?
- Do we work on holidays? What about weekends?
- How does our time off relate to our work for you?
- What is considered an emergency?

- How do we contact you over the weekend, on a holiday, or in an emergency?
- In general, when are we available for questions?

In addition to letting clients know about this document up front, every time someone e-mails us, they get an automated response that says what our protocol and procedures are for responding to e-mails. It gives the clients peace of mind because there are clear instructions about when they'll hear back. It gives us peace of mind because we don't have to worry about disappointing anyone by not constantly being available.

Business-by-design helps to give you freedom, space, and clarity around boundaries—all important things. However, what you say isn't as important as how you enforce these boundaries.

Say you tell your kids they can't have ice cream right now, but they keep asking you over and over (and over) again. Finally, on the seventh time, you say, "Fine, you can have ice cream." You just taught your kids that the key to ice cream is being persistent. The same thing is true with your clients.

You have to back up your how-we-work plan with consistent follow-through actions 100 percent of the time. If a client sends me a message outside of the agreed-upon channels, I'll ignore it. That is the only way to reinforce to someone the acceptable ways to communicate. The trick is, it's your responsibility to enforce—and then reinforce—your boundaries. In the following chapters, we're going to look at how to do just that.

TAKEAWAYS

- *Journal:* Building your business-by-design is all about setting boundaries around client communication, enforcing work/life balance, and establishing healthy ways to run your business. What kinds of goals do you have when it comes to these ideas?

- *Reflect:* What are you struggling with when it comes to the never-ending list of things to do? What are some strategies you can try to lessen the psychological load? Remember, if it was meant to all be done, it would be called a to-done list, not a to-do list!

- *Do:* The sooner you can implement a budget—and have a clear budget going into every month—the sooner you can actually leverage your money and make it work for you. Look into budgeting and see what kind of program or process will work for you.

CHAPTER 12

Make Room for Big Rocks

I always thought there would be a day when I would have hired enough, delegated enough, and said no to enough that there wouldn't be a ton of things left that felt important. But that day has never arrived. The truth is, every single client and every single opportunity is super important—or at least it feels that way. It never gets to a point where there's a shortage of things that feel like an emergency and need to be done right now.

On top of that, there's the phenomenon of Parkinson's law, which we touched on in Chapter 4. Simply put, this is the idea that things expand and contract to take up the space that's available. Say you have one room where your kids are supposed to play with their toys. There's going to be a toy explosion in that room. But if you allow the toys to be played with all over the house, then they're going to be all over the house. The result? It'll take a lot more time and effort to pick up and contain the mess. As another example, if you say you're allowed to spend up to $100 on something, you're going to spend $100—and if you say you're allowed to spend up to $1,000, most likely you're going to spend $1,000.

Parkinson's law can also influence your time management. If you say, *I'm going to get this ad campaign placed, and I'm going to give myself all of Thursday to do it,* it's probably going to take you all day. But if you take your laptop to a coffee shop, forget your charger, and only have 10 minutes of battery life left, you are magically going to get that ad campaign placed in 10 minutes.

This was me: I realized I was giving too much time to my work because I didn't have well-defined start and stop times or any other kind of boundary. I made all of my time available for work, and I used it all on work—textbook Parkinson's law.

All of this also contributed to why I didn't prioritize my health, friendships, or hobbies. I didn't delegate certain activities in my business. I was running around serving every single client who asked me to do something until I burned out. I didn't think that I could make it another year and was falling out of love with my business. I remember a late-night coding session that ended with me lying on the floor of the bathroom, crying by myself, and thinking, *If this is what the rest of my life is going to look like, I don't want to do this anymore.*

THE BIG ROCKS THEORY

At that low moment, I remembered an old illustration that my dad, a youth pastor, used to present in church. It was of the Big Rocks theory, which was popularized by Stephen Covey.

Imagine that you have some big rocks, pebbles, sand, and water. Say we're going to try to fit all those things in a vase. If we first fill up the vase with the water, when we add the big stones, the water will start sloshing out. If we start by filling it up with the sand, then perhaps we could add a bit of water before it overflows, but we wouldn't be able to fit in any pebbles or big rocks.

But there's this amazing thing that happens when you start with the big rocks. You can arrange the vase, filling it up with big rocks. Then pour in the pebbles. Not all of them are going to fit, but many will fill in around the big rocks. As you pour in the sand, it will filter around the big rocks and pebbles. And the beautiful thing is that, even though the vase seems full, when you pour in the water, some will still fit, filling every last nook and cranny.

I thought, *What if I took this analogy from my childhood and applied it to my business?*

The idea is that big rocks represent what is most important to you. These are the people, things, and activities in your life that keep you going. These are different for everyone and can change from season to season. Only you can dictate your own big rocks—and there isn't a right or wrong way to pick them. The pebbles represent things that are related to your big rocks—maybe it's a weekly appointment or an activity you do on occasion. And then you also have sand and water, which signify the rest of the things that fill up our day, such as sleeping or eating.

Always make room for what's most important first. Family is definitely a big rock. Maybe marriage falls under family or maybe it's a separate big rock. Friends might be important to you. Focusing on your health, which might also include sleep or fitness, could be a big rock. Some people consider faith or spirituality a big rock. Maybe hobbies are important to you, or maybe they will become a big rock later in life.

WHY THE BIG ROCKS THEORY WORKS

Without big rocks, there's no way to fit everything else into our lives.

Thanks to the big rocks theory, I concluded that I don't need to do everything—in fact, I can't do everything—and I can't be working all the time. The only way to be constantly available is at the expense of my sanity and my health, and it's just not worth it.

The big rocks theory was also really, really helpful in realizing that a successful business requires more than creating boundaries and following a business-by-design plan. You have to know what you want your life to look like before you can decide what you want your business to look like.

For me, in order to create a business-by-design plan, first I had to think about living life by design or creating a life blueprint. I asked myself, what do I want my life to look like? Do I want to work evenings? Do I want to have family dinners? Do I want weekends to be work-free? If your business by design doesn't fit your life blueprint (and vice versa), either you've picked the wrong business, or it's the wrong life design.

TAKEAWAYS

- *Journal:* Following the big rocks theory can help you set priorities and identify what's important to you. Consider what your big rocks, pebbles, sand, and water are—both in your business and your life.

- *Reflect:* How do you see Parkinson's law at play in your life?

- *Do:* You have to know what you want your life to look like before you can decide what you want your business to look like. Create a living-by-design plan so you can see how your work life will fit in.

CHAPTER 13

Setting Boundaries

As we talked about a few chapters ago, business-by-design is all about boundaries. Boundaries are incredibly powerful. They allow you to stay in a healthy relationship with your clients and your business. In fact, without proper boundaries, you may absolutely grow to detest your business.

What do successful boundaries look like? Imagine an open, unfenced front yard. When there's no fence, anyone can walk on the grass and ruin the lawn. That's annoying, right? But when there's a fence, things are different. People are a lot less likely to walk through your yard. It's pretty simple: adding a fence—a.k.a. boundaries—helps direct people's behavior.

Unfortunately, real life isn't so neatly defined. I'm going to speak from my own experience: it is much easier to ignore than to maintain boundaries. A lot of people don't understand boundaries around online behavior, so it can be especially difficult in social media and digital communications. And it is so easy to let clients, prospects, opportunities—really, the entire world—push you into thinking that you don't need to honor the boundaries you set for yourself.

THE THREE COMMON BOUNDARY-BREAKERS

Too often, I've found the world thinks that they deserve instant and 24/7 access to and communication with my team and me. That's not possible, it's not smart, and it's (understandably) exhausting. If I were to respond to all the notifications and opportunities and messages I received throughout the day, I would never get any work done—*ever*. I would never have weekends or weeknights with my family.

As I was thinking about the clients I've encountered in my work, I realized the people who break boundaries tend to fall into three types.

Red Flag Raymond

Red signifies danger for a reason. Red Flag Raymonds don't have good intentions and will blatantly disregard your boundaries. In fact, they only care about their own endgame. This mindset stems from greed, selfishness, and a lack of care for others. Red Flag Raymonds will knowingly break your boundaries to see how far they can get away with testing your limits. For example, if you make it clear you don't communicate on weekends and will respond to questions on Monday, Red Flag Raymonds will continually insist on calling you on Saturday.

If you encounter them, you need to run in the other direction. This type of person will continue to push your boundaries for the rest of your working relationship.

Eager Earl

Eager Earls don't realize they're violating boundaries. In contrast to Red Flag Raymonds, they have the best intentions and message you a ton only because they're excited, nervous, or uncertain. Eager Earls are not necessarily bad people. They just take a little bit of coaching on how to respect your boundaries.

I understand Eager Earls because I can be this person sometimes. To them, I tend to say, "I'm glad you're excited— I'm excited too. I will get back to you on Monday. I've got you—don't worry!"

Frantic Fanny

Like Eager Earls, Frantic Fannys act with good intentions, but they are in constant fight-or-flight mode because they're *terrified*. They've been burned before—maybe due to a tough childhood or rough business experiences—and don't trust people. Frantic Fannys are going to be checking in all the time, double-checking your work, and making sure that everything's on point. They'll probably resemble a micromanager. Take note of this type of person and decide if you want to deal with that type of fight-or-flight energy in your life and business as it often takes a lot of up-front work.

With Frantic Fanny, you'll find that calm, gentle leadership and constant reassurances help. You can say, "Hey, I'm here. I care, and I understand and hear your concerns. I'm committed to continually working on your project." If they feel heard, they will be more likely to place their trust in you.

DRAWING THE LINES

To prevent these boundary-breakers from slowing down your business, here are a few examples of major boundaries you should get in place in advance.

Manage Client Communication

Every client prefers a different method of communication, but you get to decide where and when you'll connect with them. If you don't make your preferences clear, it can become a big problem that affects your life and happiness. For example, if you consistently tell someone, "We communicate over Slack," and they're still texting you—and you're responding—that's a problem. You're teaching them that your preferences aren't important, and that they can text or call any time they need anything.

I experienced this with a client who called me on Thanksgiving and said, "I want to launch a Black Friday sale. Right now." Shocked, I asked, "You want me to put this together on Thanksgiving?" But I wasn't mishearing things: "Yes," she responded. I tried to talk her out of it, saying that there wasn't enough time or notice to create a campaign. (Plus, again—it's Thanksgiving, and I'm spending the holiday with my family.) But she insisted, so I gave in and did what she requested.

I later asked myself what was I doing answering my phone on Thanksgiving in the first place. That's when I got mad. In fact, I was angrier at myself than I was at the client. We get frustrated with ourselves for allowing someone to overstep what we want for our lives. That's even more of an incentive to define—and then stick to—your boundaries. This experience was one of many that made me realize I needed to state, clearly and directly, how I communicate with clients, and it led to the creation of how-we-work documents (see Chapter 11).

When I was a new business owner, I always thought the client was the boss. But I'll say this again: you get to decide when you communicate. I've had many clients who would text me late at night—or even in the middle of the night!—and say, "We need to get on a call now about our campaign." Today, I make it clear to clients in our initial agreements that an emergency is extremely rare—and emergencies don't include typos, an issue with social media accounts, expanding scope, or sharing a new idea. Just because something seems stressful doesn't mean it's an emergency.

If you're working a 9-to-5 job on top of building your business, it's not always possible to set the days or hours that you'd prefer working. But you can, and should, still put parameters around when and how you are available to communicate with clients.

Insist on Mutual Respect

It's important to make it clear up front how you expect communication to go in business relationships. How do you talk to people? How do you allow people to talk to you?

To avoid any misunderstandings, I have tough conversations with clients about expectations right from the get-go, a process I call preframing. You're basically telling people that when we're in a business relationship, here's what communication will look like. Personally, I communicate very directly. Most of the time, we're focused on the mission, the things we need to do, and getting the best results possible. So I'm often doing things without a lot of niceties or fluff. It's just, "Here's what needs to happen."

Now, that doesn't give anyone permission to act like a jerk. Communication should be respectful between both parties: I will respect you and expect that you respect me in return. And I'll continue to work to earn that respect. This requires honesty and trust; we're not trying to hurt each other's feelings on purpose, and we're also not taking offense or jumping to conclusions about behavior.

Let me give you an example of how wrong this can go. One of my first big clients was very high-maintenance and texted me nonstop. (I answered, of course, because I didn't have boundaries set up with them.) Ultimately, things came to a head when they called me at 2 a.m. and were like, "Are you there? Hello—answer!" And I was like, "I can't answer right now—I'm asleep!" That wasn't good enough for them. They got me on a phone call (because I let them), right then and there, and proceeded to yell at and scold me because they weren't pleased with how their ads were running. Two grown men in their 40s. In the middle of the night. (As a side note, it's true I was responsible for a $25,000 ad spend on a big launch. But we generated $1.6 million in revenue. It's safe to say their concerns were misplaced.)

I was so hurt and frustrated, and I felt like I had become a doormat. I didn't know how to grab control of the conversation, and the dynamics they were insisting on threw me off balance. I didn't know how to say, "You can't talk to me like this." It took almost until the end of the call before I told myself, "Wait a second—I'm an adult too. I can decide how my business grows, what kind of clients I work with, and how they treat me." Finally, I took back the power and told them, "This is not okay. And I'm not going to be okay with this kind of behavior."

That example was an extreme situation—hopefully things will never go that far for you! Of course, people make mistakes; there will probably be raised voices and misunderstandings. We don't have to freak out and fire everyone if they flip out on us. If you've set up your boundaries and made them clear, strive to give people the benefit of the doubt and expect that they'll give you the same respect in turn. You also want to build mutual trust and respect so that if there are mistakes or something the client is upset about, they feel comfortable coming to you right away and explaining it so you can resolve the situation.

That middle-of-the-night disaster was definitely a turning point. I called one of my coaches the next week and asked for advice. She made it clear: "Rachel, you do not need to allow this willingly into your life." That was when I determined I needed to focus on a boundary-filled business. Today, my clients and students quickly learn that most of the time I am completely unavailable in the evenings and on weekends.

You might be surprised by how setting clear boundaries can aid in your business relationships. At first when I started sending clients the how-we-work document, I was worried they were going to be mad. Instead, I was met with respect. That was *not* what I expected to see, and it blew me away. People started accommodating all the boundaries that I requested. They were like, "Oh, you're busy. You're a big deal." When I told them what I needed and expected, I started being viewed as a priority.

Be Aware of Scope Creep

In addition to setting boundaries around communication, the how-we-work document also helps me rein in one of the biggest challenges faced by business owners: scope creep, or the phenomenon where a client requests something that's not in their contract.

First things first: you can and should be getting compensated for what you do. Charging what you're worth and asking for more money is just a business decision. It should be simple to say, "I'd love to do that for you. Here's the invoice for what that's going to look like." But discussions around money can be difficult, and it's easy to make it personal. That's why, when we say yes to all kinds of things and don't set communication and work boundaries, we become resentful. When we grow resentful toward a client about their behavior, we often get angry at ourselves for not creating and maintaining boundaries and putting too much on our plate once again.

Scope creep can bring up a lot of layers of shame. It's literally a magnifying glass on all of our insecurities and past experiences. Perhaps you're afraid of being perceived as mean because that's what people have labeled you throughout your life when you say no to things. In addition, we want to deliver great service and make our clients happy.

If a client asks you to do something outside of your scope and they ask nicely, you can say, "Hey, I noticed that you asked me to do this, and it is outside of our current agreement. Do you want me to send over a proposal for what that would look like? I can totally do that for you. I'd love to." Nine times out of 10, they actually say yes; they want that proposal and the upsell opportunity. The other time, they'll backtrack and say, "Oh, I didn't realize that service wasn't included."

But it's not always so easy. Clients partial to scope creep can be very demanding, manipulative, and bossy. They might say, "I need you to do this for me right now." Admittedly, this can be intimidating. However, you have the power to flip the script in your head and say, *Wait a second. I'm not unreasonable or mean or unhelpful because I'm charging extra for services that weren't included in the original contract.* Especially if it's intentional, I like to sometimes match their level of intensity. I might say something like, "I will do it as soon as you pay the invoice." It's super important to keep in mind that strong demands need to be met with stronger boundaries. Plus, there's something really powerful if our response to a client meltdown reasserts our boundaries.

HANDLING TOUGH CONVERSATIONS

I struggle with confrontation; that's just how I'm wired. When it comes to handling tough conversations, I've learned the best thing to do is stop and take a moment to reassess. Confrontation brings up panic mode—your fight-or-flight response. When you're in panic mode, *do not have tough conversations*. What you need to do is step back, crack open your journal, and write down your feelings about what's going on. Make sure that you know exactly what you want to communicate. Let your nervous system calm down; formulate a clear plan of attack; and come back to the conversation when you're out of panic mode.

When I'm ready, I'll send an e-mail or message that clearly outlines exactly what's going on and what needs to change. I simply say, "Hey, you know, I actually don't allow people to talk to me that way. That's not the way my life is. That's not welcome to be a part of my life. So if you want to speak respectfully, you're more than welcome to be a part of my life. I'll continue to work with you. If that's not something that you can respect, just let me know now so that we can go ahead and end our future relationship of working together."

Asserting yourself like this is really powerful—and it can certainly be more than a little scary. But the best thing you can do is get in the right frame of mind and handle the tough conversations right away. Otherwise it can boil over into bigger frustrations and resentment, which can lead to burnout. In addition, if you hold frustrations inside, no one can help you solve them.

Here's another example of a boundary-pushing client. The campaign was over, and I was so relieved. But one day, out of the blue, he sent me a text message: "Hey, I e-mailed you, and it's been a week and I haven't heard back." I called him and said, "You know I don't check e-mails. That's something my team does. They must have thought the message didn't need a response, but I can check in with them about it."

He sounded surprised, and said, "You don't check your own e-mails?" And I responded, "I have to choose between being a mom and checking my own e-mail. My kids come first." The client continued to push, incredulous about the way I ran my company. "I know someone who owns a business that does $15 million a year, which is multiple times larger than your business," he explained. "And he still checks all of his own e-mails."

At this point, I was annoyed and remembered thinking, "Good for him. Is he going to come here and spend time with my kids? Or is he going to explain to my children why Mom's no longer with them every evening—because she's responding to e-mails?" Instead of arguing with him, I exuded confidence and said, "You know what, I won't tolerate being spoken to that way. If that's how you're going to speak to me, this isn't going to work."

Guess what? Although we didn't resume our client partnership, he respected me moving forward in our interactions. And I was okay with that.

FINDING BALANCE

Besides showing how I maintain boundaries, the previous example illustrates a very important point: there's a trade-off to everything. Every single yes is a no to something else. This is especially true when trying to juggle business and personal lives. Remember your big rocks? They take up a lot of space, and sometimes you have to decide what's worth keeping and what's worth setting aside.

Recently, I decided I wanted to train for a marathon. I was very excited! But what I didn't take into account is that we were about to go into a wildly busy season, both in our business and kids' activities. I soon realized that multiple things were going to need to shift completely if I wanted to make marathon training a priority. I realized I'd have no time for friends, any other extracurricular activities, or networking when I traveled to events, and, worst of all, I'd probably have to miss some of our kids' activities. I had to weigh the pros and cons of this decision. Did I want to actively say no to activities, a social life, and networking? Or, although it's something that I want to do, can I put aside my marathon dreams until later, perhaps when the kids are a little bit older?

Making these sacrifices can be difficult. But it's important to set boundaries—even with yourself and what you want, because you simply cannot do it all at the same time. In order to say yes to something, you have to be willing to look other things in your life in the face and say no to some of them—even if they are important. To name a few: Am I willing to say no to that extra hour of sleep each day? Or am I willing to say no to my health? Am I willing to say no to my kids when they want to have family dinners? Asking myself questions like these was a huge shift.

A GRATITUDE SWITCH

Clients are people you're bartering with for your dreams and your goals. You're bartering your time and your expertise (and sometimes your sanity). Yes, at times clients are nightmares. Yes, things can be out of alignment occasionally. That's why you want to make sure you have your business-by-design intact. Remember, you're bartering those things for a financial investment.

This is important to keep in perspective. And here's where something I learned from Lisa Nichols's book *Abundance Now* comes in handy. It's the idea of extreme gratitude for clients. How much are you willing to give when you realize that your clients are giving you the ability to build the life that you've always wanted? That's a really cool gratitude switch. Whether or not you work with them forever, you can be like, *Wow, this is really neat. This person is paying me $2,500 a month. That means I'm able to put $1,000 into my emergency savings fund,* or *I'm able to pay off that one credit card that's been so worrying.*

When you switch to an attitude of gratitude, your clients are not only going to stay longer, but you're also going to attract more clients. If you're always complaining about clients, they're going to disappear. People and money go where they're appreciated. So take a moment and be incredibly grateful that you have the ability to work with the clients that you are currently serving.

In the balance of money versus value, I personally try to always make sure that I come out ahead in every business transaction. Now, that doesn't mean that I am the person who is visibly taking more. Instead, I reframe this: it means I want to be the one who's giving more. If you ask the majority of the clients that we've worked with, the majority of them are going to say, "I can't deny it: Rachel gives and gives and gives, and she overdelivers time and time again." I do that on purpose. The trick is that it's going to build you a favorable reputation.

Now, that does not mean that you need to sacrifice yourself in order to give. Instead, ask yourself, "Am I giving what I committed to? And what are the little ways where I can meet needs and overdeliver?" Don't confuse this with scope creep. If I'm giving with an empty palm, then it's value. If I'm giving with expectation, it's not. If a client mentions, "Oh, I'm struggling with an e-mail schedule frequency," I'm just going to add that into the deliverables, even unasked. Or sometimes it can be as simple as introducing them to someone that they're looking for and saving them time. It doesn't have to be big.

ENFORCING WORK/LIFE BOUNDARIES

Another pro of setting boundaries is that it gives you time to actually *do the work*. Starting out, I had trouble managing e-mails because I didn't understand how to prioritize. I would often respond to every message that came in as soon as I possibly could. I felt that if someone asked me for something, I owed it to them to respond, and that every e-mail warranted a reply. However, after I found myself spending hours working on my inbox, I realized that this was taking away precious hours that I could have been working on campaigns, doing research, or otherwise leveraging my skills. I either needed a team to help me or I needed to be choosier about the e-mails I addressed.

This is *hard*. We're taught the ideal state is an empty inbox. We feel pressure to reply to every single e-mail—and reply right away. However, there simply aren't enough hours in the day to juggle this much communication. Humans aren't meant to respond to every single thing that comes our way.

When my business started growing and I could bring on help, my team and I sat down and created a list of every single touch point—or things that needed responses such as business e-mails, social media, and meeting schedules—and came up with a best-practice plan to respond to requests. Some of the questions we asked ourselves were:

- Am I going to respond to DMs on any social media platforms?

- Am I going to respond to comments on social media?

- Will I answer e-mails personally or let my team screen and identify priority messages?

- How can I juggle a busy meeting schedule?

- Am I going to allow people to ask for a 15-minute phone call "just to pick my brain"?

Prioritizing my time and actions like this allowed me to set healthy boundaries so I could focus more on the work that most needed my specific attention. This exercise will help you slow down, see the bigger picture, and decide where you can best devote your time.

Family Life and Business

You might notice that my kids are not featured in my business marketing. This is a deliberate choice; I don't share my kids on purpose. This is mostly because my dad was a pastor, so growing up, my siblings and I were often in public, and it was like, *Look at my family. Look at how we have everything figured out. Look at how great we are.* I often felt like a prop, like there was a certain way I was expected to act to be perceived as an asset. That's a lot of weight to put on kids.

I don't want my kids to feel like there's any expectation for who they should be or how they need to show up. They're their own people, and I love them so much for that. Sometimes people will say something like, "Your kids must think you're the coolest." I would love if my kids thought I was cool, but in reality, I'm the side character in their lives—and that's the way it should be!

When I present them on my platform, they become side characters. They deserve to be the main character and have the spotlight shine on them. This way of thinking helps me keep my life and business separate (for the most part) when it comes to our kids.

The same holds true with sharing my marriage online. Poul and I are quite private, but there is a mindset in business coaching that you need to showcase your relationship so people can see what it looks like. Otherwise people think that you're hiding something or that you're on the brink of divorce all the time. So Poul and I have decided on topics that are cool—and not cool—to talk about online. For example, we don't talk about our politics, our religion, or our sex life, though we will sometimes joke or wink. What is more important to us to share is how Poul supports me as a woman in business and that there is a healthy dynamic. It just doesn't need to be front and center.

If you think there comes a day when people think you're so important that they can't bother you in the evening or on weekends, I'm sorry to be the one to tell you it never happens. There never comes a point where opportunities slow down. There never comes a point when all people will respect your boundaries all the time. And there never comes a point when it's easier to enforce overstepped boundaries.

Caring about clients and the projects you're working on is a plus—it makes you good at what you do. But it can bring on extra challenges. Some people will use the fact that you care against you to try to wiggle around your rock-solid boundaries. They'll say, "I thought you cared about your clients—why don't you do X, Y, and Z for me?" Or "You can't talk to me like that; I'm paying you." Unfortunately, this still happens to me to this day. It doesn't change the quality of the work that I put out, but emotionally, it's hard.

Over the years, I've developed several helpful habits that ensure I'm able to enforce my work/life boundaries.

- **Turn off notifications on all devices, not just your phone.** The only notifications I get are calls and texts. And only friends and family have my phone number—that's a rule.

- **Build in time to completely unplug.** Taking breaks from the online world is crucial. You might try making it really hard for yourself to log in—even deleting all social media and e-mail apps from your phone. I also love to hide my phone so that I don't subconsciously pick it up and respond.

- **Maintain your perspective.** Sometimes I imagine what would happen if I went on a one-month retreat with no technology and, during that time, a social media crisis hit my brand. Being disconnected, I wouldn't know about the crisis for the month and by the time I came back online, the whole thing would probably have blown over. It would be almost as though it didn't even happen. This scenario helps me retain perspective if a perceived crisis strikes. Remember: not everything that feels like an emergency actually is one. My friend Adrienne Dorison shared something with me that changed my life. She said, "We're not creating oxygen, people!" When she said that, I recognized so many instances where I was allowing people in my life—and on social media and over e-mail—to treat me as though what we did was the only thing sustaining their life. While the truth is that, yeah, we can all stay in touch constantly and we can all follow up and get our stuff done—nothing is *so* urgent that you ever need to respond to a message or an e-mail in the middle of the night, unless maybe you are an open-heart surgeon (or create oxygen).

- **Use an auto-responder for e-mail.** As previously mentioned, every e-mail that comes into our business gets an immediate response that confirms receipt and notes that due to the volume of e-mails, we can't respond to every one. This simple act removes the stress of having to respond immediately (or at all) and sets expectations upfront.

- **Set expectations upfront.** I've said it before, but it bears repeating. When I sign clients, they are aware of exactly when I'm available and the specific channels where I will respond. Otherwise, if you tag me outside of these places, I won't be there, I won't see it, and I'm not going to respond to your questions 99.9 percent of the time.

The truth is, I'm not perfect at this. I have to continually work on maintaining my own boundaries. If I'm being super honest here, it's very easy to fall back on old habits—especially if you're someone who grew up in a traumatic environment that taught you to be a people-pleaser for your own safety. But that's not you anymore. Think of creating and maintaining boundaries as what will keep you safe now. I would resent myself, my clients, and my partners if I let my business walk all over me. And there's great power in deciding when and how we communicate with clients or customers.

As it turns out, boundaries will set you free.

TAKEAWAYS

- *Journal:* Consider a tough conversation that you are currently dealing with. Take some time to write out your feelings, questions, concerns, and so on in your journal. Let yourself wind down from panic mode before addressing the issue.

- *Reflect:* What sort of boundary-breakers have you encountered in your work? Reflect on some difficult situations or moments when you disregarded or forgot to set up boundaries. What was the outcome? What are some strategies that you can try in the future to create and maintain boundaries?

- *Do:* Make a list of the touch points in your business—everything that you currently respond to such as e-mails and social media DMs or comments. What is working and what is not? Set up some time management or delegation strategies to help you become laser-focused and get the most out of your time.

CHAPTER 14

Find Your Support System

You can't build a business by yourself. That's why it's so important to develop a trusted network. That way, if you don't have the answer to a question or the solution to a problem, you can find someone who does. A support system can offer recommendations for mentors and help with leads on clients. When things are tough, it's just helpful to have someone (or many someones) who can take turns shouldering the load with you so you don't feel alone. Whether that person is your spouse, partner, best friend, assistant, sister, mom, business bestie, accountability partner, a member of your mentorship program, or all of the above—we all need support.

If you don't have a large network, don't worry. I believe it only takes one to three focused and available support people to get you back on course. Enthusiastic friends and other cheerleaders are excellent, but when the going gets tough, you are going to want some quality support and advice you can lean on. Here's where to start.

PEERS

By peers, I don't just mean friends or other people in your age group. This is more about people who understand your industry or are walking a similar path. For example, I have a group of girlfriends who are all business owners. We message every single day to support each other or help solve problems.

A few years ago, I wasn't sure what type of business events I wanted to host to connect with my community. Events can be time-consuming, expensive, risky, and exhausting. One of my friends in this group helped me to identify what I wanted to achieve with these events and what kind would work for me and my audience. She helped me realize that the ability to impact more people with intimate events was the direction I wanted to go. I ended up creating workshops and masterminds that focused on education.

PARTNERS

No matter how rough things have been in my business, Poul has supported me. I didn't understand; I mean, I had the track record of a failure-to-launch. Why did he believe in me? For a long time I honestly thought that he, like my mother, had to believe in me, as if being my husband meant his opinion didn't count.

But Poul sees me as my best self—and my highest-potential self—all the time. One of the things I love about him is how he always focuses on what matters. He reminds me that external change doesn't mean anything. Instead, internal change is the best option for making things happen. He would probably suggest I never do my hair and makeup because he's like, "It's just not necessary. It doesn't change your heart." Outside of business, Poul is also my favorite person in the entire world. He's my best friend; he is home. He is the place where I can truly be myself, let all my guards down, and not have to worry about what anyone thinks. And vice versa.

I'm the only Rachel Pedersen. Poul is the only Poul Pedersen. We're the only couple that is just like us; every single relationship is completely different. Don't take my marriage advice or try to make your marriage fit this mold just because it works for us. You have to know what works for you and your partner. I'm also not trying to tell you my marriage or my partnership is perfect. We do the best we can, and that's all we can do.

STRANGERS-TO-SUPPORT

After Poul, Jeannie and John Buttolph were the first people to believe in me and my vision—and it all began one day over a head of highlights. I was newly married, pregnant, and working as a colorist in a hair salon.

Jeannie's stylist had canceled last minute, and I was able to fit her in. From the moment this bubbly blonde in her 50s sashayed into the salon—because Jeannie didn't just walk anywhere!—I had a good feeling about this chance encounter. This woman was clearly confident and fun, and she made jokes and put me at ease throughout the entire process of explaining what she wanted. As I started doing her hair, she was chatting away with me while working on something on her cell phone. She seemed incredibly confused and frustrated. Finally, she asked, did I know anything about Twitter?

We started talking about social media, marketing, and business—at that point, the extent of my business knowledge came from reading a few personal development books and watching *Shark Tank* religiously. I told her how I posted about my services on social media and people magically came in to see me. It always felt like social media worked, though I didn't always understand how. Jeannie shared with me that she and her husband had just purchased a fast-food chicken franchise, Mrs. Winner's Chicken and Biscuits, and they needed help with marketing. She asked me if I'd be willing to work as their marketing consultant on an hourly basis.

The answer was yes!

I went home and told Poul all about it like a giggly little schoolgirl. Someone besides him had seen my potential! Several weeks later I went to their house, and I was so nervous, waiting for someone to pull the rug out from under me. But, sure enough, it was a bona fide job. I met Jeannie's husband, John, and they became my first real clients. I was a marketing consultant! I helped them set up all of their social media accounts, develop marketing strategies, and create and post content for their social media platforms.

Eventually, they invited Poul and me over for dinner, and the Buttolphs raved about my work to him. On the way home, Poul was beaming with pride. He said, "Babe, I'm so happy someone else gets to see you the way I see you."

I had never met people who believed in me so much. It was like John and Jeannie saw who I could be before I even saw it. At that time, I had lost faith in a lot of my aspirations. I was just doing what I could to keep on going and keep getting by. But their support and belief instantly changed my trajectory, and it didn't stop there.

John invited me into the world of restaurant professionals, took me to industry events, and introduced me to people. Jeannie taught me how to convey confidence, craft an e-mail professionally, make people feel heard, and take action on big tasks without getting overwhelmed. It was hands-on instruction. Jeannie once brought me the book

Vision to Legacy, which is about a Great Clips hairstylist becoming the CEO. She looked me straight in my eyes, and with a stern voice so I wouldn't miss what she was saying, said, "This reminds me of you. You could be a CEO one day." Up until that point, I didn't have a consistent voice in my head telling me that my skills were valuable and I could do more. It was like they were continually planting and nurturing seeds in my life.

Although I was later unsuccessful opening the Mrs. Winner's franchise in Memphis and felt like I let the Buttolphs down, their belief was unwavering. The truth is, for the rest of my life, I will be grateful to them. Their belief was exactly what I needed. I've never seen love in action so strongly. Their belief was love in action.

TAKEAWAYS

- *Journal:* Who are the people in your community whom you can rely on? What kind of support do you already get? What kind do you need?

- *Reflect:* Sometimes we don't realize how much we take on by ourselves. Where are areas where you're taking on too much? How can you ask for support if you need it?

- *Do:* Make a list of things you can ask your support groups for help with. Perhaps you have a technical question you've been struggling with, or maybe it's more about big-picture dreams for the future. Then, go out and make your asks.

CHAPTER 15

The Power of Mentors

A mentor is a person who can guide you through any concerns or questions, both personal and professional. Finding a mentor who has walked the path that you want to walk and successfully come out on the other side is invaluable. Their experience can give you proven, tried-and-true solutions—not just hypothetical advice.

I absolutely love mentorship. Every mentor of mine has taught me something—even the bad ones (more on that later). I've learned how to save money, make money, pay less in taxes, hire smarter, and be a better leader. I've gotten advice on marketing and advertising strategies, relationships, home buying, organic social media, and more. A good mentor will nurture you with encouragement and advice as well as provide constructive criticism when it's necessary. They can help you troubleshoot issues and identify common mistakes so you can fast-track success.

How Do I Find a Mentor?

- Searching on YouTube, TikTok, or other social media for people answering the questions you have

- Look for books that answer your questions

- Sign up for trainings from industry professionals

- Ask people in your industry, such as your support group or an online community

- Go to industry events

But before you engage with a mentor, you need to know exactly where you want to go. If you don't know what you want from life or business, you're not ready for a mentor. Most mentors can't help you figure these things out. In fact, it's not their job to help you figure these things out. Only *you* can put in the work needed to define your business idea or vision.

Once your business starts generating significant revenue, you might start paying mentors. However, I recommend starting out with free mentors and mentorship options. This puts less pressure on the situation, especially because you might not know at first whether someone's going to be a good fit for you or your business. When you invest financial resources in a mentor, it often involves business contracts—and you do not want to join with a mentor, then have to cancel your contract or ask for a refund if the relationship doesn't work.

FREE MENTORSHIP OPTIONS

Let's talk about what to do when hiring a mentor isn't an option. You might not have the time, resources, or ability to tap into a network or simply are not in a place to hire a mentor. If this is you, embrace the idea of mentoring from afar.

Oprah Winfrey, Shonda Rhimes, Tony Robbins, Roland Frasier, Perry Belcher—there are so many different people I want to learn from. Luckily, many successful people have free interviews of varying lengths that you can watch on YouTube. I frequently learn from successful people by watching these types of interviews.

If you're not quite ready to hire a mentor, this can also be a good way to get an idea of how they work and what their expertise is. It's like a kind of trial run. You can learn a lot about who people are from their presentations. Plus, they also often share the precise steps that they took to get where they are—so have your notebook ready! In addition to watching videos, you can read their books and blogs, get on their e-mail list, take screenshots of interviews, and generally just study everything they put out there. You never know when it's going to come in handy or provide inspiration.

I know it's not the same as hiring someone to coach you personally, but reading and listening to speeches can be a great way to crawl into someone else's brain. So grab a snuggly blanket and a cup of coffee, and savor the ability to peek into the lives of some true legends.

Joining a mentorship program with an amazing community—in business, this is usually called a mastermind group—means that you will have access to support, advice, and expertise from both peers and leaders all the time. In these groups, you'll often be connected with people who are further along their journey, which is incredibly helpful for major growth.

However, I do not recommend asking a free group for serious business advice, especially if it's for legal or financial reasons or serious decisions. Free groups have no buy-in to your business. You also have to be wary of trolls, people with different moral compasses, or even competitors hoping you fail.

From time to time, you may come across the opportunity for free one-on-one mentorship, though this is not usually the norm. I've only ever had one mentor—Jay Abraham—take me on for free. He said, "I want to help you grow. I think you're amazing. And all I ask is that you connect me with some other really amazing and awesome people." Of course, I was happy to connect him with different friends and share his content and expertise in exchange for free mentoring.

The free mentorship model has pros and cons. Before agreeing to be mentored by someone for free, make sure they've achieved what you want to achieve. Just because someone's willing to be your mentor for free doesn't mean that you need to take them up on it. I've discovered that the people who are the quickest to offer up their services for free are not necessarily the people you'd want to mentor you. They might not have much experience or could even be looking to take advantage of you.

WHAT ARE YOU LOOKING FOR?

Once you're clear on your vision and decide you are ready for a mentor, then your job is to find someone who understands your desired path to success. That's why the first thing to do is look for a mentor who has either achieved what you want to achieve or helped a ton of other people do the same.

A good mentor is basically like a fantastic GPS. This person is familiar with the journey that you're about to go on, and they can help you get through the potholes, traffic jams, and detours that will happen. There will be problems; there will challenges; there will be things that fall apart. That's why you want someone who knows the path.

You will often receive exposure, connections, or expertise from a mentor's network, so choosing a mentor who surrounds themselves with people you'd like to connect with is a great idea. A few years ago, I joined an Inner Circle mentorship group of Russell Brunson's, whose work I admire immensely. Being a member was really important to me, because I knew that Russell was connected with people who were successful in business, and I wanted to be in proximity to those people to learn from them and network. I ended up being connected with not just millionaires, but also multimillionaires and even a couple of billionaires.

In addition, when I had a huge business setback in 2017 after having my third child, I went to a mastermind of his with tears, heartbreak, and tons of humility. They helped me create a plan that fixed everything in just a few months. So having these types of connections can be lifesaving.

Another thing to consider is that you might not need or want a long-term mentor. A short-term mentoring relationship can also make an impact. For example, one time I got a text message intro from someone I really respect, Roland Frasier, to Jay Abraham, an absolute legend in the marketing and business space. Jay and I had two amazing phone calls—and that was it. Although it wasn't an ongoing mentorship, Jay taught me a fantastic business acquisition strategy that I will tap into someday soon.

Before hiring a mentor, do a thorough look into their life and behavior, focusing on these three categories.

The Way They Show Up

Read testimonials from other people they've mentored. See if they come from people like you, people who are looking to achieve similar goals. Also get a feel for how they are live, because some people are very different when they have to think on their feet rather than follow a script. Watch unscripted trainings or Facebook and Instagram livestreams so you can hear how they handle different scenarios.

The Messaging They Use

Do as much research as you can on their messaging: content, tone, how it's presented, everything. Go through their YouTube channel, books, and free resources such as their blog or e-mail newsletter. Do you relate to what they're saying and the way they're saying it?

How They Make You Feel

Ask yourself, does listening to their content make you feel more whole? Or does it make you feel afraid or full of uncertainty? Do they give free resources that help? What is the quality of their free advice? Can you use it to get results?

SETTING EXPECTATIONS

The next big thing I want to share—and this is big—is how to set your own expectations so your experience as a mentee can be a success. There are a few things to keep in mind.

Most mentors are going to do things their own way. Very, very, very few mentors are going to operate within your business-by-design. Plus, not every mentor is going to give you one-to-one attention. Mentors are busy, and they might be giving out advice to multiple people on top of juggling their own work. So if individualized advice is what you want, make sure that is something they are willing to provide.

It's also important to keep in mind that it's not the mentor's job to carry you. Whether you paid for them or they're free, you still need to do the work. Imagine that your mentor is a marathon coach. This coach can tell you to run faster or slower, what shoes to wear, how to move your feet, what to eat, and when to drink. They can help you with everything—except actually running the race for you. The question you want to ask yourself is, will they able to motivate you and give you clarity on what your next steps are?

Before hiring a mentor, ask them questions such as:

- What time are the calls?
- Are there one-on-one calls, or does mentorship happen in a group setting?
- On an average week, how often can I expect to hear from you or talk to you?
- What are the things that you help your mentees with the most?
- How many of your mentees fail to reach their goals? And what is a big reason why they fail?
- How long does it take for your mentees to see success?

Don't consider these intrusive questions; these are important questions. A mentor's response is going to help you clarify what your relationship will look like. For example, if someone tells you that all of their students see instant success, you might want to ask a few more questions to clarify what they mean. No mentor is ironclad. No one has a 100 percent success rate or sees instant results, and if they tell you otherwise, you probably want to steer clear. Look for answers that feel honest and give you a good feeling about the mentor and their methods.

Four Good Types of Mentors

The cheerleader: This is the one who makes you feel like you can do anything. As long as they're in your corner, you've got highs, you've got energy, you've got someone rooting for you. They're audibly fighting the voices in your head that are saying you can't do it.

The drill instructor: This mentor is straight-up going to give you the harsh, barking truth. This approach isn't always right for everyone, though it works really well for certain personality types. The drill instructor is very powerful and can help you get out of a slump.

The motivational sage: This mentor will rarely tell you what to do. Instead, they're going to ask you questions that help you bring out the truth you already know. I love when you get a good mentor of this type, but they are so, so, so rare.

The true leader: This is the one who is forging a path similar to yours. They're literally setting the example and doing exactly what you want to do. You get to follow in their footsteps. They're paving a path, making it possible and easier for you, and they've got your best interests in mind.

ASKING QUESTIONS

Once you've vetted and chosen your mentor, now it's time to get started. But what do you ask them? Sometimes people will ask mentors basic questions such as, "How do I upload a video onto YouTube?" I don't like to ask those kinds of questions because if it's an answer I can easily google, I don't want to waste that mentor's time. When you ask your mentors better questions, you'll receive better answers.

Here are the different iterations of questions I like to ask mentors:

- Here's what I plan to do. What pitfalls should I look for and avoid?

- Here's my vision. What's the logical next step—or next couple of steps? What would you do first?

- Here's where I'm going. In general, what would you tell me about this path?

- I want to do this. What advice do you have for me on that path?

- Who do you recommend I connect with? This is what I'm looking for.

What do these questions have in common? Besides being open-ended—meaning they're not yes-or-no questions—every single time I'm offering information on where I'm planning to end up, then asking for advice.

A great example of this is when I was completely stuck about how to bring my business to a new level. I was able to ask my then-mentor Russell Brunson, "Hey, if you were me, what would you do to achieve this goal?" And he said, "Here's what I would do—X, Y, and Z." He gave me the next steps so that I could take action confidently in the right direction.

Another thing to consider: if you're going to make an investment, make sure that you see the return. This is super important, whether you are hiring a mentor or working with someone for free. After all, in the latter scenario, you're giving your time, which is also valuable. Commit mentally to taking action and doing the work a mentor asks of you until you see a return. This could look like personal or professional growth, or a specific improvement in results such as leads, reach, sales, engagement, and opportunities.

RED FLAGS

Red flags are things you want to watch out for that might signal something is not right with your mentorship. For example, if a mentor says, "Do as I say, not as I do," that's a red flag. If a mentor tries to make you feel bad for getting opinions from others before making a decision, that's a red flag. If they put high pressure on you, saying you need to make a decision now or else you'll never be successful—run. This is a dangerous sales tactic. Mentors who try to use fear to control you do not have your best interests at heart, and they can be dangerous.

In the past, I have also had mentors who tried to tell me what to do and where to go with my life. Not only are these mentoring relationships a bad fit—they also end up being completely unfulfilling. Remember, you are the one in charge of your dream and your vision.

And then there was the time I found out that a mentor betrayed our business.

It was 2017. In addition to running a marketing agency that had just reached a million-dollar run rate, I was CEO of another business that was doing six figures in revenue per year. At the time, everything seemed to be going great on paper. We were winning more than we were losing, most of our clients were happy, and we were generating healthy revenue. Our business partner, a former employee we had promoted and brought in as acting CEO of the marketing agency, was making more from the partner profit payouts than he ever had as an employee. We had also hired a mentor to help us scale our business. In fact, he was the one who recommended we promote our current business partner. All told, we were paying for both businesses to receive mentorship, to the tune of $5,000 per month.

Poul and I were enjoying a rare moment of relaxation, hanging out poolside in Jamaica during downtime from a marriage conference. I got a dreaded three-word text from the business partner—"Can we talk?"—that instantly sent chills down my spine. When I responded, he immediately gave his notice, saying that he needed to leave the company.

Poul and I were shocked and blindsided. The partner was quickly becoming one of our best friends; we treated him more like family. We celebrated our kids' birthdays together, traveled together, exchanged Christmas gifts. What happened?

After we spoke with him later that night and asked some pointed questions of our mentor, it seemed clear that our mentor had poached our business partner.

After we met this mentor for the first time, Poul admitted he had an instant bad gut-feeling. Poul is very perceptive like that. But we ignored red flags because the mentor won us over with his charms. He said all the right things, did all the right things, and came recommended by all the right people. So we brushed off our gut feelings even though it was a clear indication of his character. When we confronted them, both parties were adamant that there was no poaching going on, and the now ex-mentor even warned me to be careful what I said about the situation going forward. But poaching was exactly what had happened.

I still believe in mentors, but my process is a bit different these days:

1. I look for their current mentees and ask them about their experience.
2. I do a background check on them.
3. I double- and triple-check the contracts and even include a non-solicitation and non-compete clause.

The entire experience was hard, but it was a reminder that not all mentors are created equal. If a mentor—or any business partner—is making you feel as though you should always be afraid, as if you aren't capable, or as if gloom and doom are literally lurking around every single corner, that's a really good sign that they are leading with fear. This can cause a negative ripple effect in your entire life and business that leaves you worse than before you started to work with them.

That was one of the biggest red flags from that bad mentor that I just didn't catch.

Of course, not every mentor is going to be the right fit, and that's totally fine. If you're in a place where you're able to invest in mentorship, it can be an amazing game-changer. Find a mentor you trust who has a good track record and is kind, supportive, and strong.

TAKEAWAYS

- *Journal:* What sort of questions would you like a mentor to answer about your business or business strategy right now? Spend some time writing about what's coming up for you when you consider your current challenges.

- *Reflect:* Looking at the four types of good mentors recommended in this chapter, what kind of mentor would you want? What qualities do they have? What kind of support do they offer you?

- *Do:* Whether you're ready to go out and hire a mentor or not, there are lots of opportunities for free mentorship from hugely successful people. Make a list of people you want to learn from and go find videos or other resources that they've made available.

CHAPTER 16

Every Business Journey Is Different

I remember inspirational posters that hung across the walls of school classrooms saying things like, "Dream big and shoot for the moon—at least you'll end up among the stars." At the time, I had a love/hate relationship with those posters. Part of me felt like they were incredibly cheesy, but part of me loved them because they reaffirmed this belief that I could be myself and also have success. I loved that concept because when I was a kid, I was quite the individual. I wore the wildest outfits: a big pink tutu or a princess dress with cowgirl boots and a hat to match. My imagination would run wild, and it felt like the world was my playground. A box could become a spaceship. Or I could become the next president of the United States. There were no limits.

But over time, I began to realize the idea that you could be yourself *and* simultaneously be successful wasn't necessarily true. Growing up, I watched my parents and so many others follow "the plan" for life. This plan includes getting a degree, having 2.5 children, getting a house in the suburbs with a dog and a cat, and working your way up the corporate ladder, hoping for a promotion every two or three years. I never saw them follow their gut or make decisions based on love. These moves were always based on fear and calculating or reducing risk.

I was also taught to always look your best, hide your mess, and play the part. Say what people want to hear and make them happy. Those were very clear messages that were pounded into my head as I grew up. I always had this underlying fear that if I let people see who I really was, I would be completely disowned.

As an adult, I became very nervous, always waiting for the other shoe to drop. I worried that someone would see a video of me being silly or take one look at my super bubbly and goofy self and judge me—people had been hard on me for that in the past. I also worried that if people saw me like that, they would challenge my expertise, my work ethic, and my desire and ability to learn. People who have known me for years—my husband, family, team, friends—would all tell you I'm a very nice person. Being nice is important to me, but I was afraid that if I was assertive, someone would say, "See, I knew you weren't nice all along."

I was so afraid of people making snap judgments about me and deciding I wasn't serious enough or good enough to hire that when it came to my job, I left my personality behind. I became a crusty professional—stale as a box of saltines that's been sitting on a shelf for way too long. In e-mails and copy, I stopped using exclamation points. When I got my nails done, I asked for "something classy but intelligent," meaning a plain French manicure. I even changed the way I talked. I'm a goofball, and that no longer showed in my conversations. I put together a polished résumé and dulled my sparkles so that I would fit in with others. I started wearing blazers and carrying a briefcase-handbag hybrid so everyone would think I was a pedigreed professional.

I don't even *like* blazers. So why did I start wearing them?

PROFESSIONALISM IS KILLING CREATIVITY

Somewhere between Jeannie's pep talks and building a multimillion-dollar business, I became terrified of being exposed as unprofessional. It seemed like the worst label in the world, so bad that it was worth entirely changing who I was to avoid it. And then, I fell out of love with marketing and business. I wasn't having fun anymore. I felt as though I was pretending to be someone who I never was going to be. (Man, the price of pretending takes a toll on your energy!) I even wanted to quit marketing, the thing that I love.

Although I went through all this years ago, I've discovered that this fear of unprofessionalism continues to be a serious issue. I've heard similar sentiments from coworkers, bosses, prospective clients, and even team members. I've been told repeatedly to be less, to not seem so excited, to not be so bubbly, to not make a fool of myself.

Have you ever been told that you're too much? Or that people don't take silly girls seriously? Have you ever been passed over for an interview, a job that you really wanted, or even a promotion, because of the way you dress or any other aspect of how you define yourself? Maybe a job has told you to tone down your personality. You may have been told to use fewer emojis, no exclamation points.

You're certainly not alone. I went to Google to see exactly what advice was being given to people who are looking for jobs, promotions, or other new opportunities. I found that 65 percent of bosses said that clothes could be the deciding factor between two candidates with similar qualifications and 70 percent of employers claim that they don't want applicants to be fashionable or trendy.

Something didn't sit right with me about those percentages. I decided to google "How could I be most likely to be the best candidate for a job?" There was a lot of very interesting advice, but most of it was offered underneath this one umbrella: how to dress. How to dress right for an interview, how to dress right to get a promotion, how to dress right in the workplace. That was funny for me, because I thought, *Who decides what's "right"? I didn't know there was a wrong way to dress to be successful.*

Another response from a college recruiter said to avoid anything excessive, which included but is not limited to, and I quote, "flashy jewelry, sparkly eyeshadow, bad ties, bold ties, colorful patterns, and fun socks." In fact, their overarching advice for anyone who wants to get a job, be promotable, and have success in their career is to wear a suit. Part of this is thanks to corporate culture—which was built by white men, meaning they were seen as the standard for what a "professional" should look like.

But what became most clear to me is that professionalism is killing creativity. (I actually gave a TEDx talk on this, and you can find it on YouTube.)

Today, we put the burden on people looking to advance in their career by making it important to ask, "How do I dress right for a corporate success story?" But what we need to do is start laying the burden on employers. The question that should be asked is, "How do we find amazing talent despite how it fits the mold of conventional professionalism?"

I started to think about how many people I know who are wonderfully, wildly, remarkably talented in different ways. I thought about people who have winged eyeliner, natural hair, tattoos, piercings, bold fashion. Creativity comes in many packages.

Résumés and work histories cannot paint a full picture of people's zones of genius. They don't explain what these employees might do if given a chance or show the surprising life experiences that shape them as a worker. Sometimes incredibly talented people have employment gaps, which of course don't tell the whole story. Maybe they took time off to care for a child or a loved one or to focus on school.

TRADITIONAL IS OVERRATED

It's no wonder so many people leave a 9-to-5 job and start their own businesses. This path offers more room for nontraditional careers and work histories.

The best hire I ever made came in with an unorthodox background. When I was pregnant with my youngest child, I became overwhelmed running two businesses, making all the decisions by myself and trying to manage a team. Even though I was pulling all-nighters and working 100 hours a week, I was somehow always falling short.

My husband, Poul, stepped in to help. More precisely, he knew he needed to help, but he felt underqualified. Before I started a business, he was a high-school dropout who had a GED and later worked as a window washer. More recently, he had worked his way into the automotive industry as a service writer for Mini Cooper vehicles. Poul took over hiring, firing, finance, payroll, budgeting, events, and sponsorship negotiations.

Now, I would not have naturally assumed that Poul would become crucial to the business in this way because his résumé didn't show any inclination toward these roles. However, he is absolutely brilliant. When Poul stepped in, he took on all the stuff that drained me. I was pregnant and exhausted at that time, and my depression was kicking in hardcore. He filed contracts, led the team meetings, and handled events, logistics, bills, credit cards, and travel plans. All the things I'm not good at. This freed me up to do things like write a book, create videos that inspire people, and work with our amazing clients. I basically have the front of house, and he has the back of house.

Personality-wise, Poul is also so brilliant in his role because he's very logical, rational, and fact-based, meaning he makes decisions based on his principles. These traits are crucial for the finance side of a business. And so even if he didn't have the exact experience before jumping into this role, he could follow his strong values and his principles to make the right decisions. Poul allows me to get so much more done than I ever would have alone. In fact, this is the only reason that I'm able to keep growing the way that I do. We both have a mutual understanding of our goals and mission in life, and we take turns supporting each other to do it. It's not even just about who's watching the kids. It's literally like, "Hey, let's check in. Who needs some time away to recharge, go take a bath, or walk on a treadmill?" We literally take turns as much as we can in life and in business.

There's another example of this in my executive assistant, Kellyanne. She worked as a server in a cafe before working with me, and we've known each other since we were in high school. (Fun fact: when I was a hairstylist, I did her hair for prom!) I took a bit of a gamble on her as my executive assistant, but she's grown into an incredibly capable EA.

She's organized and on top of things and looks out for my best interests; her main goal is to protect me in the business by not letting all my time and space get eaten up. However, Kellyanne also really and truly cares. Recently, we hung out late and had an amazing night together. But she said, "I would not ever take this type of job for anyone else." She said if she was working for anyone else, doing the same exact thing that I'm doing, she would hate it. Kellyanne has to care about the person she's working for. And she really, really, really cares about me, and vice versa. We're like sisters.

There are also many advantages to going nontraditional when it comes to work. One of the byproducts of the COVID-19 pandemic is that, for the first time, many businesses became more accepting of nontraditional work schedules and offices that were remote or hybrid. It's wild to me that it took a pandemic for workplaces to understand how difficult work/life balance is.

One of the best decisions we made in our business early on was giving our team the ability to work from anywhere on their own schedules. If you want to play in a softball league, you're welcome to catch up on work after practice. If your kids' school is canceled for the day, get back to us when you can. Being understanding about situations such as health appointments and occasional Fridays off can make a huge difference for worker happiness and retention.

People get great work done from home—you're probably an example of that! If you allow them to embrace the flexibility and freedom of the best schedule for their life, you'll be amazed by the talent you can attract.

THE ELLE WOODS EFFECT

When hiring and considering workplace culture, the last thing any good business owner should want are robots: assembly-line automated humans programmed to perform a task that was designed a long time ago a certain way.

I love creating amazing, powerful strategies that grow a brand and help it become more profitable. I especially love using some of the really cool trends that are available on social media. But I don't love creating PowerPoints, having to type up reports, or spreadsheet anything. I know I'm not alone. But I constantly see companies asking wonderful creatives and visionaries to waste time on PowerPoint presentations or filling out spreadsheets.

Instead of trying to make someone fit the mold of one personality or process, successful employers should account for different personality types and let workers be themselves. Humans act differently depending on the situation, and stressful conditions are not conducive to creativity or success.

It's also easy to overlook that you will get amazing opportunities not *in spite of* who you are. You'll get amazing opportunities *because of* who you are. After years of being afraid to show my full self to clients, I finally asked myself, *What if I just decided to be me all the time?* I decided I didn't have anything to prove to anyone And I made a promise: I'm just going to be myself.

For this shift, I credit Reese Witherspoon's character in the movie *Legally Blonde.*

Poul agreed to watch it with me, and I *sobbed* through the movie. I was leaning over to him through tears saying, "Poul, did you hear that?! She is so nice and bubbly, and no one understands her!" and "See! You can be smart and goofy!" and "Why did I ever stop wearing pink? Elle Woods proves it's okay!"

Watching the film felt like a spiritual experience. I realized that somewhere along the journey to growing my business I forgot that we win most when we choose to be ourselves. When we hide who we really are, people sense a disconnect between our true selves and who we're pretending to be. They assume we're hiding something and see red flags. When you're unapologetically yourself, you never have to worry about being found out. You're just you, all the time, no matter what.

I remembered all of my strengths. I'm incredibly intelligent, I'm a quick reader, and I'm very good at learning—my memory is almost photographic when I decide to turn it on. I also really, genuinely like communicating and connecting with people. When I sit down and talk with people, everything else fades away, and I have these amazing heart-to-hearts where we connect deeply.

After that *Legally Blonde* viewing, I started the process of rediscovering myself and showing my true self to clients. I was amazed by the opportunities that opened up. Several years later, I decided to get a neon rainbow manicure and color my hair platinum before flying to Arizona to consult for a major client. I wore fun outfits and told silly stories. I was exactly myself, and you know what? They hired me.

TAKEAWAYS

- *Journal:* Are there any people—whether in real life or in characters such as Elle Woods—who really inspire you to be yourself? How do those people act even when they're seen as less-than by others? How do they prove people wrong?

- *Reflect:* Where does your business have the potential to incorporate nontraditional aspects for you, your team, or your clients? Are there traditional things in your life that are holding you down?

- *Do:* Take a hard look at the way you are in your daily life and your professional life. Are you being your authentic self all the time? If there is a part of yourself that you're suppressing due to fear, start working on it. Wear those funky shoes. Do the colorful makeup you like. Use exclamation points.

CHAPTER 17

The Power of Daily Improvement

In early 2020, I received an e-mail from someone subscribed to my e-mail list. They simply asked, "Do you want to give a TEDx Talk?"

Do I want to give a TEDx Talk?!?! Yes! It's only been on my vision board for six years! I had, in fact, submitted a TEDx pitch just the previous week—and then I got this e-mail. Unfortunately, I ended up not being able to give my talk live; many TEDx events were canceled due to the pandemic. Though I really missed the energy of a live audience, we made the most of things. We set up an area in our basement with red LED lights to give the feeling of being on a live stage, and I wore a colorful, cheerful skirt.

The day we were set to film, my two oldest kids stayed home from school with fevers and a nasty cough. My youngest was at Grandma's house for the day, also sick. And, of course, I was starting to catch what they had, as I felt my throat getting sore and the dull ache of a fever. We planned on recording later in the day, but I was hours away from being down for the count. Missing this TEDx Talk taping wasn't an option, as I had a hard deadline to turn it in. I got it done and despite all the issues, it turned out great. (It's the talk I mentioned in the last chapter, called "Professionalism Is Destroying Creativity.")

We've all been here: when everything is going wrong, sometimes you just need to push through. But that doesn't mean it's easy. Sometimes you just don't feel like doing anything or are not physically able to run at full speed. In fact, I have consistent weeks or even months where all I want to do is forget my workload for the day because it's gloomy outside. I want to eat mint chocolate chip ice cream, put on a Marvel movie marathon, and relax. Everyone has days when the motivation never comes, or you're too tired to lift a single finger. How about when you've got your period and you're bloated and emotional? Or when issues in your personal life make it feel impossible to get any work done?

Getting out of a rut isn't always simple, although some people claim there are quick fixes. For example, I have heard people abuse the relationship with vision, saying, "If it's something you believe in, you'll find the reason to wake up every single day. If you have vision, it will always be easy." However, this is a rose-colored view of vision. That's like saying, "If you love your kids, it will never be hard or tiring." I love my kids, and I can easily say that not every single day is roses and sunshine.

Sometimes you do need to take a break—and that's okay too. But there are times when that's not an option. Because of my depression and anxiety, if I wait until I feel better, I will have missed all the deadlines for the entire week, which only adds to my anxiety as I stress about disappointing customers and dropping balls both in my professional and personal life.

In this chapter we'll look at strategies to help you move forward through daily incremental improvements. Making a difference comes from doing things consistently over time because you're creating good habits that help you make good decisions in the long run.

TAKE ACTION STEPS

Getting from where you are to where you want to be can feel like a massive challenge. Not only do you not know what that path looks like—how rocky or steep it is or what kind of obstacles are on it—you might not necessarily be able to see all the steps it will take to get from the beginning to the end.

You can't tackle big tasks with a single step, just like you can't scale a mountain with a single bound (unless you're Superman, of course!). So the magic comes from splitting those big tasks into smaller tasks that can be accomplished in one go. I call these action steps. You can use these incremental action steps to make your path easier. And you don't have to know every single step along the way to get started.

Think about *The Lord of the Rings*: Frodo and his friends didn't know what they would encounter along their journey—they just knew that they wanted to save the Hobbits and mankind. If they knew everything that was going to happen in advance, would they ever have left the Shire? Maybe not.

When they took a step, they would come up against different challenges. And they would take a moment and say, "Okay, we need to get to the other side of these mountains. I don't know if we can go over the mountain pass, but we can go under the mountains." Was it safe? No, not necessarily. But they focused on asking, "What is the next step we can take that will keep us going in the right direction?" When everything feels super big, when it feels as though you don't even know where to start, focus on the immediate future. You don't have to see every step right away. You can instead say, "What is one step I can take today that will help me to get there?"

It all adds up over time. First, it's just taking action. But then you can review your action steps and the results and ask, "Can I just do it just a little better?" Tweaking things a little bit at a time over time will keep you on an easier path to your goal. You can see things that might be going wrong and can fix them before they completely derail you. Before you know it, you become a pro. One day, you'll look back at your journey and be like, "When did that happen?" I saw that so clearly with TikTok: people literally made fun of me for my videos—but now they're all asking if they can hire me, and my prices are too high for them.

FOCUS ON DAILY PRIORITIES

If you're still feeling overwhelmed, it can help to break down your day into three daily priorities to make sure that you're taking the right action steps. Ask yourself, "What are three things I can do today that will get me one step closer to a bigger goal?" It might be reaching out to clients, following up with leads, and connecting with a potential mentor. Once you know what those next couple of steps are—the most important thing is you take them.

Let's be real: many of the action steps that you take day-by-day—at work, at home, at the gym—don't feel great in the moment. Maybe they even feel crappy. I rarely finish an action step and think, *Wow, this is amazing*. When I first started producing YouTube videos, it all felt like a bunch of short, tedious action steps to get those videos out. I had to set up all the equipment, map out the script or at least the general flow, shoot the video, do reshoots, get it edited, upload it, add keywords, do formatting . . . The list went on, and it often felt never-ending. Even as I wrote this book, I got down 500 words and was like, *That was mortifying.* But I just continued to move forward, write more, and take a bunch of little action steps. This doesn't describe my attitude toward these things—I love doing them all, and seeing the finished product is so rewarding—but rather how it felt in the moment.

BUILD ENDURANCE

You also have to focus on what steps are accomplishable for you—with your skill set and the resources you have available at this moment. Take exercise, for example. If you're looking to exercise more and you don't want to spend money on a gym, you might try running. When you first start running, you get tired quickly. Maybe it's only three minutes before your legs are burning and you need to take a break. You can basically still see your house—you feel like you've barely gotten anywhere! But running, or any kind of exercise, starts out as a bunch of little steps, and you build endurance as you practice. So tomorrow you run for 5 minutes, next week for 10. It's not until you realize how far you can go months down the road that suddenly you're like, *Wow, I'm doing it. This is fantastic.*

FIND BALANCE

Assessing your priorities can expose the dualities of your life. On one side is this thought: "I need to care for myself and my family; practice self-care; and recognize when

I'm burning out." But then there's the other side: "What do I want to achieve? Who do I want to become? What do I want to make happen in my life and in my business?" Trying to find balance between both of those sides is key.

On days when I'm finding it difficult to get anything done, I create an MVE pact with myself. MVE stands for both Minimum Viable Effort and Minimum Viable Energy. I outline the work that absolutely *needs* to get done that day, then the Minimum Viable Energy I need to spend so I don't miss anything crucial. There is always pressure to work when you're building a business, but by making it clear exactly what needs to get done, I ensure I don't spend any unnecessary or extra energy.

This is when my Power 10 comes in handy (see Chapter 4). This list of tasks is the bare minimum that I can commit to getting done no matter how I feel and reflects the Minimum Viable Effort I can give. I use my Minimum Viable Energy to get everything on my Power 10 list done that day. Then I give myself permission to rest. Usually this MVE Power 10 list takes between two and four hours, so I can be productive before taking the rest of the day off to rest and do what I need to do to recharge. Interestingly enough, when I finish my list, I will often get a second wind from momentum. Accomplishing things—even small things—feels good!

As I'm going through an unmotivated period, I will also usually take some time to ask myself some important, tough questions about why I'm feeling like this today. I like to take a moment to reflect and write in my journal, a judgment-free zone.

WHEN YOU'RE SICK

Of course, if I am really sick with the flu or another illness, I'll take the day off to recuperate. If I am exhausted and know my body is asking for sleep, I might take a relaxing bath or rest for a few hours. On sick days, I don't have my Minimum Viable Energy. However, I still ask myself honestly, are there any deadlines that I'm committed to meeting?

If so, I ask the people who I committed to if it's okay to get them the promised work in a couple more days. Sometimes they say yes, and I have more time to finish. If they say no or don't respond, I get the work done, because I want people to know my word is my bond. Most of the time, people are going to say that it's totally fine to take a few extra days. But there will be times when you're sick and still need to get work done. You can find balance even in these kinds of situations.

In our agency, I work one-on-one with big clients who have high expectations of me. One of my clients does $100 million per year. One time, I was super sick with the flu and a fever around Christmas and said to this client, "Hey, I'm really sick today, so I'm not at my best. Could we move this to next week? If not, I'm happy to honor it today. But just know I'm going to come across a lot less energetic." And they said, "We can't do it next week. We need to do it this week—today—in order to hit all of our goals and deadlines." I showed up and gave them the energy that I had so we could keep things moving. I also let them know that after the call, I would be going to sleep and couldn't be around for any additional conversation or work.

As another example, when I was finished recording that TEDx Talk and made sure I met the deadline, I quickly changed into a sweatsuit and lay on the couch for the rest of the day. MVE is a powerful tool to use when things get tough.

MAINTAIN FOCUS

As you move forward, you're going to see many rec-ommendations for what you should be doing. There's all these people saying you have to have a YouTube presence or need to be on TikTok or need this specific kind of mar-keting tool. Though it can be helpful to hear what others find useful, all these opinions are distracting and might make you lose focus.

The truth of the matter is, the most important thing for you today—and on any day—is to consider what you need to do for *you*. Make sure the action steps you're taking are moving you toward your specific goal.

Consider your goal. Maybe you'd like to be able to have dinner at a nice place a few times a month. Maybe you want to bring in some support on your team, hire some-one to clean your house, or to say yes to your kids when they want to do something fun. With those bigger, specific goals in place, start breaking down how to get there. You can secure more clients or increase your revenue to reach your goal. So, you make a plan to gain two to five new cli-ents and consider an increase in your rates. How do you go about finding new clients? What kind of increase might be workable? Break it down into doable action steps; that is all you need to focus on today.

Don't let the world sway you and make you think X, Y, or Z is important when what you need to do today is A, B, and C. Focus on what moves the needle for you, your fam-ily, your life, and your business. Ask yourself: What are the most important things I need to be doing today toward my goal? And focus on your priorities.

TAKEAWAYS

- *Journal:* If you're feeling unmotivated, grab your journal and do some freewriting. Consider questions such as, *Why am I feeling this way today? Why do these tasks feel unsurmountable? Am I running from hard work that I know needs to be done?*

- *Reflect:* In your day-to-day life, how do you already break things down into smaller tasks to get them done? Doing laundry, going to the library—almost everything takes multiple steps. How is this process already second nature to you?

- *Do:* Create action steps for what you can specifically get done today to move yourself, ever incrementally, toward your goal. You might try the Power 10 method to help yourself focus.

Part IV

PASSION AND PERSEVERANCE

CHAPTER 18

When Things Get Difficult

A few years ago, I went on vacation and completely disconnected from 99 percent of the social media world, taking a few days to spend some time with my family and clear my head to get back on track mentally. One of the things I did on this trip is (surprise, surprise) spend a lot of time reading, including *Shoe Dog*, a book about Nike's formation and growth by the company's creator, Phil Knight.

Reading about the journey of building Nike was shocking to me. There's an assumption that big companies have massive funding and that everything runs smoothly; that there's a tipping point where everything gets easier. But Nike was started back in the 1960s and still wasn't profitable until shortly before they reached $140 million a year in sales.

At every single step along Knight's journey, there were peaks and valleys. I would think, *Oh, they've got it now. This is the point in the book where everything's going to happen— they are about to have a massive breakthrough.* And then, all of a sudden, a torpedo would hit the business: a $25 million customs tax bill, a hostile takeover, their manufacturer trying to sabotage their growth, or competitors ganging up on them.

It gave me some excellent perspective. I was like, *Wow, here I am sometimes being frustrated about something that doesn't go right or according to plan.* Yet Nike went through decades of trials and huge setbacks. The massive, wonderful, profitable breakthroughs only happened in time, thanks to hard work and dedication. It is so beautiful to read about legends such as Phil Knight. Their business lives, and even sometimes their day-to-day lives, are peppered with failures, mistakes, setbacks, challenges, and things that go completely wrong.

CHOOSE A PATH

Ask any highly successful person and they will all tell you *absolutely* things will go wrong. Even when you're doing well. For example, in late 2020, I hosted a two-day event where everything started falling apart. Within 30 minutes on the first day of the event, all the tech that had previously worked fine suddenly malfunctioned. On top of that, one of our tech people suddenly became super sick with COVID-19.

In that moment, there was a part of me that was tempted to just cancel everything. That was the point where the old version of me would have given up. It would have been easier and I could have just said, *Well, I guess it wasn't meant to be.*

But then I thought to myself: *Wait a second, I'll never know what could have been if I cancel this.*

Challenges, mistakes, failures—all those things are absolutely inevitable. When I'm facing issue like thiss, I like to imagine I'm standing somewhere and see two paths in front of me.

One is the path I don't take, where I will never know what could have been. The other one is the path that leads to every good, great, and wonderful thing.

It's *your choice* which one you walk down. With every single challenge—every single no, every metaphorical door slammed in your face—you get to pick the path. Across every memoir I've ever read, the one thing that the authors have in common is that they kept going. They didn't know if there was going to be a massive payoff. They didn't know if everything was going to work out. They didn't know that their companies could potentially go public and make millions and then billions of dollars. Regardless of what trials came up, regardless of how bleak the future looked, regardless of mutinies or hostile takeovers, they believed in their idea and kept going. They never allowed failure to be a legitimate, viable option. They persisted, no matter what happened. They just kept taking one step, another step, and yet another step forward again, even when they didn't see a clear path to the success they imagined.

Chances are, you'll also experience something where you'll think: *This is too much for me.* But when you fall in love with the journey, the trials, challenges, and things that make us wonder, *Why am I doing this?* suddenly become an amazing part of the daily adventure.

PLAN FOR BUMPS IN THE ROAD

In business, things will eventually go wrong. Trust me on this: it's not a matter of if—it's when. How you respond to these challenges and curveballs is what matters.

Planning for bumps in the road can involve being proactive by having preventive measures in place. I think of these as runaway ramps. If your brakes give out, you need to get off the road because you will become a danger to yourself and others.

An excellent runaway ramp is your profit and loss statements. You need to go over your books once a month so that if things are starting to shift in a direction you don't like, you can make the appropriate adjustments. People think businesses that have troubles just spend a little too much one month and then suddenly everything goes wrong, but that's not usually how happens. There are usually multiple checkpoints where red flags could be caught, but you have to be looking for them.

However, there are some instances when no amount of planning will help. For example, a client might fire you. What do you do then? Grieve however you need to, go write about it in your journal, then get back to work. That is going to be a normal part of your business forever. You might also have an out-of-control client. First go vent about it to a friend or therapist. Determine whether the relationship is irreparable, and if it is, let the client go.

Then trace back your conversations and discover whether there were red flags that you ignored. Chances are, most of the time you'll find some. The best thing you can do when the dust from a bad situation settles is to make sure you learned a lesson from the mistake. A mistake is only painful and expensive if you don't learn a lesson from it. Otherwise, it's an investment.

When a team member messes up, someone drops the ball on something, or a freelancer ghosts a project, it's okay to be angry. But get your anger out before you talk to that team member. Go run on a treadmill, punch a punching bag, throw some weights around. I'm not saying to suppress your rage, but you cannot have an ounce of rage when you talk to that team member. Remember, it's your job as the business owner to take ownership for everything, including the actions of that employee.

Of course, there's only so much planning we can do to avoid possible problems. You can't predict everything that might go wrong. In fact, you could be handed all the answers to life, business, and every single challenge that you're ever going to go through, and you would probably still not listen to all of it. Why? The value of these answers comes in experiencing the challenges firsthand and understanding the consequences.

Experiencing these consequences isn't necessarily a bad thing. For example, if you kid doesn't clean their room and their friend comes over after school, they might be embarrassed because now their room is messy. They might be like, "Mom, what am I supposed to do?" And you'll shrug and say they should have cleaned their room earlier. Facing consequences helps you learn lessons.

The same thing is true in our businesses. If you're seeing the same challenge coming up over and over and over again, it's time to step back and ask yourself some pointed questions.

- When am I actually going to deal with this?
- What is the root cause?
- Is there something in my blind spot?
- Is there something I'm not showing up for in the right way?
- What lesson is here for me to learn?
- Is the solution a skill set that I need to develop?
- Is this an area that is going to continue to come up?
- Is this a one-off, weird incident?

When life presents you with those inevitable challenges, think of it as an opportunity to develop your skill sets and your strengths. Every single one is a potential lesson to your future self that says, "Hey, listen, this is an area that you're going to want to develop. This is going to come up again and again until you learn it." In other words, challenges also help identify weaknesses and flaws, which means you can then fix them.

The beautiful thing about business is it's a mirror for life. It's a mirror for our personal lives, our mindset, what we think about ourselves, how we view the world, and how we view relationship dynamics. And so when your business hands you a challenge, you're literally being given a mirror that magnifies everything that's already there. It says, "Hey, listen, there's a big old blackhead right here. Can we take care of this so it doesn't permanently enlarge this pore?" You're being given the ability to develop, to grow, to leverage strengths, and have honest, meaningful conversations.

WHO IS THE ADULT IN THE ROOM?

When our former mentor and business partner betrayed my trust, as painful as it was, it helped me learn one of the greatest lessons of my life: stop looking for the adult in the room.

You see, the reason I was so messed up by the mentor's betrayal is because I was expecting him to be the adult. Though I was 30, had three kids, and owned my own business, I still had this mindset that I was a kid, that other people knew better than me. Since he seemed to have things figured out and spoke with more certainty and authority than me, I figured he was the right mentor for me. He was clearly the adult in the room.

After that whole situation, I posted a Facebook status to my page: "What was the best advice you've ever received?" When I asked the question, I was genuinely excited to see the answers from people I trust and respect. And they didn't disappoint, contributing advice that encompassed tough love, smart life insights, and simple-but-brilliant inspiration. Nestled in the middle of these answers was one response that forever changed me. A follower quoted an advertising agency CEO who said something along the lines of: "Stop trying to find adults, because nobody has any idea what they're doing."

At first, I stared at the advice, mildly offended. It hit so close to home; was this aimed directly at me? But then it clicked, and I started laughing. While there may be some exceptions to this advice—for example, someone who has dedicated years toward achieving mastery in their area of expertise may have some idea of what they're talking about—most people don't know what they're doing. This is everyone's first go-around at life. Anyone who says they "have it all figured out" is straight-up pretending.

Reading that advice, freedom washed over me like a cool rain after a long, hot run. It was like I had new eyes and could more fully understand the actions of so many people. That phrase—stop looking for the adult in the room—kept popping up in my mind, and I even started thinking about how it related to many of my previous bad experiences. I realized that what happened with that ex-mentor didn't occur by accident. He knew *exactly* what he was doing. The situation occurred because I was looking for the adult in the room everywhere I went. I put the mentor on the "grown-up pedestal" and assumed that since he was the adult, I would be safe.

What's funny is that otherwise, I was the adult in every single area of my life from being in control of household decisions to taking control in the doctor's office. I was capable and confident telling my family, friends, and other people outside of business what was best for my life. But in some situations, I just couldn't help but look to other people to be the grown-ups.

Even writing this today, it feels a little ridiculous to admit this. I was clearly not a kid, yet I was acting like a child in the presence of specific people. By constantly looking for the adult in the room, I was subtly declaring that I didn't value my own thoughts, opinions, and decisions.

If you're looking for an adult to make the decisions, remember: it's you. You're the adult in the room.

You can make a decision.

No, you don't need to weigh anyone's opinions.

Yes, it'll be okay if you make a mistake.

Potentially, you'll be able to course-correct if it's the wrong decision.

Absolutely, people will begin to see you as the adult in the room if you act like one.

Before you know it, people will begin to ask you for your advice, opinion, and expertise.

TAKEAWAYS

- *Journal:* Do you act like the adult in the room in all situations in your life? When are you looking to others to make decisions or not valuing your own thoughts and opinions?

- *Reflect:* Think about a time when you were stuck facing an obstacle and needed to choose a path. Which path did you choose? How did it turn out? Did it bring you closer to your intended goal? What might you have done differently?

- *Do:* Make a plan for potential bumps in the road. Maybe it's a routine evaluation of P&L statements. What do you foresee as issues that might come up? How can you plan ahead?

CHAPTER 19

Overcoming Obstacles

People say to me all the time, "Rachel, I'm so uninspired," or "How do I find the motivation?" or "I lost my passion." These three things—inspiration, motivation, and passion—are important sparks that get you started. But they won't sustain your fire without some extra effort.

FROM SPARK TO FIRE

Let's start at the beginning:

Inspiration is the spark for creative endeavors.

Motivation is the spark for action.

Passion is the spark for absolutely loving something or someone.

At the end of every episode of the reality TV show *Survivor*, the contestants all place their votes for who is going to leave the island. Sometimes there's a tie, and this situation will trigger the infamous "fire challenge." The two contestants have to start a fire that burns bright and tall so it burns through a rope that's two feet above the fire. Sounds simple enough, right? But here's the thing about the fire challenge: contestants often think the only trick is getting the fire to start burning. They don't spend time *planning* their fire.

What happens next is entirely predictable. Contestant One grabs all of their kindling, throws down some sticks, and lights it up. Their fire blazes bright, and it looks as though they're winning for about 10 seconds until the lack of structure causes it to burn out just as quickly as it started. Contestant Two, who spent a minute or so building a solid base for their fire, may not have gotten it lit as quickly, but their fire is then able to burn higher and sustain that level long enough to burn through the rope. Contestant Two wins because they thought a few steps beyond the initial spark and were able to make a fire that was up to the task.

Now back to inspiration, motivation, and passion: consider those three qualities as fire starters meant to help you start a blaze with a solid foundation. Then, you can build onto that fire and have a much easier time keeping it lit. These fire starters won't help you keep the fire burning continuously, but they are crucial to getting you started. You need more than sparks—you need fuel, which comes from things such as vision, self-discipline, and commitment.

Here are a few real-life examples of what this looks like.

Inspiration was the fire starter for writing this book because I have so many ideas that I want to share to help others. But having a clear vision for my goal creates the long-lasting fire that keeps me going. In the future, I can see even just one person reading it and experiencing a drastic transformation—and that's my goal.

Motivation was the fire starter for exercising because I want to be healthy and feel my best. But choosing self-discipline (the kind that can only come from yourself) is what keeps me going. It's why I choose to show up at the gym each day and commit to running even when I'd rather just flop on the couch and watch TV. It's a small sacrifice, but being self-disciplined means choosing the hard path.

Passion was the fire starter for my relationship—I love Poul, and we had an exciting, whirlwind romance soon after we met. But choosing commitment is what keeps me going. We decided to build a life together and have committed to making that a reality, and that's why our marriage is strong. We choose each other every single day.

Next time you are looking for inspiration, motivation, or passion and they seem to have deserted you, just remember this: those three things were what started the fire and made it easier for you to see the next steps, but the spark is not enough. You need to choose vision, self-discipline, and commitment to keep you going toward the life that you've always dreamed of.

KEEP THE FIRE BURNING

A lack of inspiration, motivation, or passion is just one obstacle to overcome as you're growing a business. When you have a really big dream, everything can seem terrifying and overwhelming. There's too much to get done, there's no time to shower, and there's never enough coffee. Without a business-by-design plan, you can easily experience burnout, failure, fear, and feeling like things are out of your control. Here's how to approach—and overcome—these all-too-common obstacles.

Prioritize to Avoid Burnout

In the past, I would get every single thing done for every single person every single day. I said yes to everything and everyone, overloading my plate and completely filling my calendar. This is a surefire recipe for burnout.

When I went through a period of burnout, one of the hardest parts was realizing that I couldn't just go pack up and go sit on an island for a month. Being a business owner, family member, and human meant I still had demands on my time every single day—demands that couldn't be ignored. Kids had to go to school. Meals needed to get made. Appointments needed to be kept. People had to be paid. As much as I wanted to hide and not face anyone, the realization that I couldn't quit everything made shifting my priorities even more urgent.

I started saying no, and I enlisted my team and my husband to help me say no. They almost protect me from myself. But I realized that the things I needed to do weren't going anywhere. Nothing was going to get better if I didn't face it head-on and start to dismantle the expectations I built around how and when work needed to be done. It's like looking at an overgrown garden and having no clue where to start—you can barely see where any of the plants begin or end. The only way to start is to face it and get rid of all the stuff that doesn't fit the vision.

If you're in a season where you can pull back and take some time off to rest, I one thousand percent recommend it. Everyone needs to take breaks sometimes. But the reality is that it isn't always possible. I couldn't just take off because there were important things—such as people's paychecks—that required me to show up. And that is one of the toughest lessons about a business-by-design. I was hoping I'd launch one program and it would sell a million dollars. And then I'd be able to say, like, "Oh my gosh, now we can take a break or whatever." Instead, I realized there was no one coming to save me.

The way I got through it was by intentionally and honestly going through every situation, client, project, and process and ask: is this aligned with our vision? No. Okay—it's got to go right now. It's almost as though we Marie Kondo'd our business. A part of that was firing a bunch of clients that were taking up a lot of my time, which was hard. But we had to look at everything and make difficult choices about what was truly important. What can we reasonably get rid of without it having a drastic impact on payroll?

Overcome Your First Big Failure

One of my first (and biggest) business failures came when I overestimated the audience for an online course I decided to build. At the time, I was still in my 9-to-5 job, but I ran a Facebook group about social media marketing and management that had around 1,000 members. I had heard so much about six-figure and seven-figure launches, and I was like, *I'm going to launch my own course. It's going to be awesome.*

I created a course about how to make your LinkedIn profile work. The price point was unbelievable: $25 for a course with 12 modules, and it included a full LinkedIn audit by me.

I knew very little about marketing but figured 1,000 people in my group meant 1,000 people were going to buy it. I thought this would become the equivalent of a six-figure launch. So I launched it and promoted it and promoted it and promoted it. I was so excited.

And I sold the course to five people.

I was devastated because I thought that the course was going to be my golden ticket to getting out of my 9-to-5. But it didn't even pay for my video editing software. I created this whole course based on what I *thought* people needed, not what they *actually* needed. I didn't even do the math properly.

There's always going to be failure. In fact, there's going to be failure every single day—a lot more failures than you ever thought possible. By the time you become successful, you will generally have some respect for people who have also become successful because you'll know what it takes to actually get there. And we all have something in common. Every single one of us has weathered failures, mistakes, problems, setbacks, challenges, lawsuits. But we've not let these things stop us. We just kept on going.

Trust Yourself

When our mentor poached our former business partner, the betrayal put me into a deep, dark hole of depression. Naturally, I felt hurt, inadequate, angry, triggered, disrespected— you name it. As a result, our business revenue tanked for the next few months as I was enveloped in a fog of doubt and insecurity. I felt so uncertain as to which way was up, who I could trust, and how I was going to get out of it.

I take ownership for my own fallout from that year. However, I worked hard to recover. In the year after the partner departed, I relied on a few select people—including authors, entrepreneurs, and friends—to help me navigate truth and business. Here's why those trusted people were so special to me. They taught me to trust *myself.*

It was a powerful reminder: you do not need cold, hard proof of someone's bad behavior to listen to your gut. Trust yourself. If something feels totally off, or you're uncertain about why something or someone feels wrong, you don't need to wait around to find out why. I used to spend so much time overriding that gut feeling. I wish I had learned sooner that "I had a gut feeling" is absolutely reason enough to make a decision, with no explanation owed to anyone else.

Realize What You Can—and Can't—Control

A lot of people give up when they encounter business setbacks. For example, I was not the entrepreneur that I needed to be to open that franchise of Mrs. Winner's Chicken & Biscuits. When something out of my control came up, I shut down, and that was the end. But one of the best things you can recognize early on is that when you're running a business, many things will be out of your control.

A successful entrepreneur can even embrace the fact that a lot is out of their control. And they're going to say, "I'm going to find out what is in my control, and take action. I'm going to say that's not a problem; it's a challenge." When you reframe your problems into challenges, you can instead look for solutions (see Chapter 3).

Embrace Fear

I used to think if I could just get rid of my fear and uncertainty, it would be fantastic. I could do anything. But things such as change, uncertainty, and fear aren't going anywhere. Instead of wasting energy fighting them, learn to embrace them. They are officially going to become your road-trip mates, so you might as well get comfy for the ride. This is easier said than done, of course. So here are four strategies I've found that help me.

1. Play the Worst-Case Scenario Game

Fear is very helpful in business because it allows us to develop courage. However, facing fear when you're experiencing it is a different story. We hold all these terrifying worst-case scenarios in our head, allowing them to spiral in our brains unconsciously. Fear plays in the background like a Hans Zimmer soundtrack, amplifying the tension.

This is the moment to verbalize what it is that you're actually fearing. Chances are, it's a hypothetical situation that's never going to happen and it's taking up a lot of your energy. When we let our fears run wild, we don't take risks and will end up missing out on opportunities. So to change my mindset, I play what I call the worst-case scenario game.

I write down the absolute worst thing that could happen, whatever I'm fully dreading. If absolutely everything goes wrong, what would that look like? Then I look carefully at all the components of the situation my fear has constructed and realize that, in reality, that's actually not even close to what would happen.

I mentioned earlier that the day Poul left his 9-to-5, I went into his workplace, put my head on his desk, and started crying and begging him to stay at his job. His job was our last safety net and the worst-case scenario was running through my head. I was suddenly so afraid that if my business didn't take off, all of my clients were going to leave immediately and we would suddenly have no money. We wouldn't be able to pay our bills. We would be evicted. And then we'd be unable to feed our kids. We'd have to make fishing poles out of sticks and go to a local hardware store and steal some fishing hooks so that we could possibly catch fish from the river for meals.

It seems a little silly, right? But that's where my fear was going. That's what my nightmares looked like. All this irrational fear was centered on this idea that we were going to end up homeless, living by the river with our children. So I wrote all of it down: we lose our house, we end up homeless. We have to fish for food and purify water over a local dumpster fire. We wash our clothes in the ocean, and our kids learn from the land.

Now, it's a little scary at first to articulate it. But the good news is, you won't die just from getting it out of your head; that doesn't make it real. You're just writing it down instead of letting your subconscious mind spiral out of control.

Next—and this is crucial—write down the steps you can take before it gets to the worst-case scenario. For example, I never stopped to consider that I could apply for a full-time job again or take a temporary position at a place like Starbucks or Taco Bell until I landed a position in my field again. I could ask family to move in with us for a month or two to help with the rent and household expenses. If needed, we could also apply for government assistance. Okay, so, now my worst-case scenario is about 100 steps away.

When I let myself panic, the worst-case scenario blots out all the other reasonable possibilities. Playing this game can be really helpful to identify and, more importantly, vocalize the irrational thoughts going through your head. Teaching yourself to slow down and get out of that mindset is a helpful part of growth and learning how to face fear.

2. Imagine Your Funeral

This sounds super morbid, so stick with me here. What would you want someone to say about you at your funeral? What do you want your obituary to say?

This is an actual question I break out at dinner parties. It's an excellent way to get conversation started or to break the ice when you're getting to know people. It usually makes people laugh uncomfortably at first. But then they get quiet and start to think deeply about their lives and what they want to accomplish.

What do you want to experience? What do you want to try? Where do you want to travel? Who do you want to work with? Who do you want to meet? What honors do you want to achieve? Can you create a list of dreams that propel you forward?

Starting with the end in mind is another way to get perspective on what you're struggling with right now. And, truly, this is a really moving exercise. Whenever I'm being too hard on myself, I remember that my obituary isn't going to say, "Her laundry was always folded, and she was skinny."

We are all mortal, but when you're bogged down in the day-to-day details of getting things done, it's easy to forget. This exercise is a quick way to provide massive perspective.

3. Drown Out Doubts

When the voices of doubt dominate my mind, I drown them out with positivity. This includes motivational tracks on YouTube, encouraging music, audiobooks, affirmations, even healing soundtracks. This strategy is more of a temporary coping mechanism, but it's effective.

Here are a few things that I listen to loudly when doubt is trying to tell me to give it all up.

4. Create an Imaginary Adversary

Have you ever felt as though you perform best when someone is doubting you or when there's an adversary you have to overcome? If this sounds familiar, you're not alone; in fact, this is common with athletes.

NFL quarterback Tom Brady was considered by many as the GOAT (that acronym for "greatest of all time"), so I started studying him. Even though playing football might not have a lot in common with running my specific business, this is an excellent lesson in letting everything and anything be your teacher. So how did Brady do it? How did he break barriers and continually grow? How did he continue to win, even past an age where people said he shouldn't physically be able to? One tactic Brady used was turning someone (real or imaginary) into an adversary. On the field, it was another quarterback, Peyton Manning. Brady pretended Manning was just this terrible person (which he's not), and it helped him to have this built-up adversary in his mind that he had to show up against.

Now, I'm not a huge fan of real-life enemies. However, there is something to the idea that when things go wrong or you're facing a tough situation, you can motivate yourself by creating an imaginary adversary. This isn't just a composite placeholder for all the collective villains, adversaries, and enemies in your life—it can also represent other negativity you've experienced.

My imaginary adversary is a conglomerate of all the terrible things people have said to me. People who have said I'll never amount to anything. People who tell me I don't know anything. By creating an imaginary adversary built from the voices that attack every doubt, fear, inadequacy, and insecurity I have, I get revved up. I want to wake myself up and prove that person wrong.

A great example of this in action came from legendary competitive bowler Pete Weber. He's about to win this big championship, and as soon as he bowls the final strike, he looks at the audience and gets super intense. Then he screams: "Who do you think you are? I am!!!" Here's the wild thing. He was shouting to an imaginary heckler. Pete Weber made up a pretend enemy who was sitting in the audience heckling him and telling him he'd never make it. And at the end, Weber was so proud to have beaten all those voices of doubt and insecurity, he couldn't contain himself.

Even though it was a cheesy, weird moment and a lot of people made fun of him (there's even a pretty famous gif of it), I understand why the imaginary adversary worked. Now, I want to make an important note here. An imaginary adversary shouldn't be a long-term coping mechanism, and it shouldn't drive all your decisions. But when we're faced with a high-stress moment, we can imagine there's an invisible tormenter in the room. Think about what that person is saying to you. How do they get in your head and make you say, *You know what? I'm going to show you—watch me. You're wrong.* This imaginary adversary becomes the thing that you can resist. When you come up against fear, doubt, unkindness, people saying, "You'll never be anything"—all those icky things—you're able to get perspective on what's really going on and react in a healthier way.

TAKEAWAYS

- *Journal:* What sparks you: What gives you inspiration, motivation, and passion? What are the vision, self-discipline, and commitment behind those sparks that will keep your fire burning and take you to the next level?

- *Reflect:* What kinds of feelings are brought up when you consider your funeral? Does it make you fearful or anxious? Why do you think you feel that way?

- *Do:* Create your own playlist, whether that's music to pump you up, inspirational podcasts and talks to inspire, or meditations to calm.

CHAPTER 20

Surprising Things about Running (and Growing) a Business

If you read enough advice books, you'll run into business gurus who basically say, "I was just sitting on my couch all day and decided to spend three days meditating, and then *poof!* A check appeared in my mailbox!"

Maybe this is some awesome synchronicity that I haven't tapped into yet. But growing a business and getting that check takes hard work. It takes discipline. It takes commitment. You can't just sit and meditate and visualize and assume that everything's going to happen. When I started studying people who are wildly successful, I discovered their secret was that they just kept plugging away at things. It wasn't like every single thing they did was a huge success, which really surprised me. Instead, they followed a series of action steps that built up and led to success. And, even when they failed or something went wrong, they just kept going.

I saw this in my own business after receiving a YouTube plaque for reaching 100,000 subscribers. We didn't have tons of viral videos. We just kept producing them several times a week, meaning each one just felt like another drop in the bucket. Over the course of six years—with two-and-a-half years where we were very intentional about our content—we reached that milestone. It didn't feel like we ever hit a grand slam with our YouTube content. But it reaffirmed for me that this was how success is for everyone. Although a business or brand might seem like an overnight success from the outside, from the inside, that success is the hard-won result of a lot of effort.

Running my own business has brought up both good and bad surprises, benefits, and perks, and no shortage of unexpected insights. Here are some other surprising things I've learned along the way.

REVENUE IS NOT THE SAME AS PROFIT

When you first start out as a freelancer or solopreneur, bringing in revenue is awesome and exhilarating because it's almost all profit. This means that most of it goes straight into your bank account. You're so excited: "Look at me—I'm making six figures!"

Of course, when you start to make multiples of six figures, you'll need to hire a team and start paying for different things that add up really fast: payroll, insurance, business-related expenses, travel. Suddenly you'll realize that revenue is not the same thing as profit. Nor should it be, if a company really, truly wants to grow.

When you hear business owners talking about awesome revenue numbers, remember that they are working with experts to manage their finances. It's not like that money is going straight in their pocket; most of it is going back into the company or to pay for expenses. Entrepreneurs hire accountants to help them figure out the best way to navigate salaries and expenses for tax purposes. For example, my CEO salary is actually well under $100,000, as is Poul's COO salary. We also don't fly in jets or rent oceanside property on tropical islands on the regular. However, we do travel first-class when flying for business, since it's a tax write-off.

YOU MAY OUTGROW OLD RELATIONSHIPS

You might have heard the phrase "It's lonely at the top" in relation to successful people. And while it seems like a cliché, it *is* lonely at the top as you become more successful, especially if you're growing a business along with a family. More than likely, you're going to outgrow some friendships and relationships.

Part of this is just how life goes, as I'm sure you've experienced. Sometimes you'll discover you just don't vibe with a person the way you used to. Maybe your priorities no longer line up. Maybe you'll discover that some of the people you used to be friends with are now very negative. (Maybe they've always secretly been that way, but you just didn't really notice it before!) In some cases, your friends might leave you because success can be really intimidating to other people.

In other words, it's okay and even natural to outgrow friendships, even if it's painful. On the plus side, however, even as you're losing old friends, you're opening up space in your life for people who align with the new version of yourself.

Of course, you don't *have* to outgrow every friendship. I still have quite a few friends from 5, 10, or 20 years ago, people who knew me way before I had my own business. Some friendships can grow as people grow, and it's a beautiful thing when that happens. But don't always expect you'll get along with the same friends over the decades. You're constantly becoming another person, and so are they.

THE DAILY WORK CAN BE EXTREMELY BORING

Sometimes people ask me, "What's it like knowing millionaires and billionaires, traveling so much, and speaking on stage?" Believe it or not, those things are like the eggnog of my life: though they are delicious and so satisfying, I only experience them a couple of times a year.

My list of regular daily commitments is incredibly long, and it can be repetitive at times having to plug away and constantly grind out content. More than once I've thought, *Ugh—I already did five videos about Instagram last week, and I want to talk about something new, like speaking French!* That doesn't mean I don't love this work—I absolutely do, and I wouldn't change it for anything. It's important to me that what I do provides value to people everywhere. But this work is also intense and consistent.

However, one way I cope is to romanticize the boring hard work. For example, when I'm writing an e-mail to my list, I always imagine I'm *Sex and the City*'s Carrie Bradshaw, sitting in her New York City apartment wearing a glamorous outfit. The truth is, I'm *not* very fashionable or chic, and I'm definitely not single in a big city. But pretending I am makes creating the same kind of content over and over again a little bit more fun.

And whenever I start to think, *Oh, this is boring. I wish my life had more chances for spontaneity and random things,* I also think about the legends and greats that have gone before me and how they became successful because they did things that other people weren't willing to do. Pro athletes often talk up their commitment to fitness and prove it through action: they show up early to practice to do the boring exercises over and over and over again. I'm reminded that if I want to be someone who has an impact on others, I still need to do those boring, repetitive things.

PEOPLE ARE GOING TO BE MEAN— FOR NO REASON

Now, I am immersed in social media, so I should have realized this point sooner rather than later. But I wasn't prepared for how mean people could be. And I'm not talking about criticism or constructive feedback like, "Hey, you know, this doesn't really work. Maybe try doing it this way instead." I'm talking about people who are straight-up willing to say nasty and negative things that will blow your mind.

You have to learn to ignore this, which is a hard lesson. What's helped is me realizing that these mean people treat everyone around them like that. In fact, I feel bad for them. Why are we worried about these people not liking us? They don't even like themselves!

Plus, you need to accept that there will be people who don't like you, no matter what you do. It doesn't matter how you show up. It doesn't matter who you are. It doesn't matter what you're offering. It doesn't matter what you believe in. It doesn't matter how nice you are. Again: *There will be people who don't like you, no matter what you do.*

For example, many people say I'm very bubbly and perky, yet oddly calming. And yet there are some people who can't stand my voice. In fact, you'll see them on every single video on YouTube giving me a thumbs down. But I've accepted the fact that there are some people who really just don't like me because I like to be silly and positive and keep things fun. I'm not going to tone myself down for someone else. You might as well live boldly in your own way and show up exactly as you are—speaking your own truth and you own message, in your own voice.

You know, I went to the bank a few years back and tried to deposit other people's approval to pay my mortgage. It didn't work—big shocker.

A POSITIVE MINDSET GOES A LONG WAY

You can't outwork a crappy mindset, at least not long term. Fighting your own negativity for extended periods of time will take a serious toll on your overall wellbeing. I highly recommend investing time and even money into focusing and training your mind.

It seems like a weird idea at first—why does my mind need training? Exercising your body is something you have to consistently work at to maintain. Your mind isn't any different! This process may include meditating, mindfulness practice, vision work, visualization, positive self-talk, and affirmations. I do all these things. I rely on them quite heavily in my morning routines to prep me for the (sometimes) boring hard work that we're going to do throughout the day.

THERE ISN'T A WHOLE LOT OF TIME FOR HOBBIES

My priorities include Poul, myself, my kids, my faith, and our business. I've had to let a lot of my hobbies go to keep these priorities in focus. Some people may think that's unhealthy, but I realized that family and business were pretty much the only things major things I had time for.

I take 100 percent of evenings and weekends off for family time and relaxation, except when I'm in a sprint. Although I'd enjoy it, I don't have time for hobbies such as painting or gardening. In fact, the one time I went to Home Depot and bought seeds for vegetables, and I discovered my thumb was *incredibly* green. We ended up with 220 thriving plants, and I quickly realized that gardening wasn't exactly a good "weekend hobby." What keeps me going is that I know there's going to be an entire lifetime after our kids become adults when I can absolutely pick up some awesome hobbies.

MONEY WON'T MAKE YOU HAPPIER

This is a simple truth that many have said, and yet so many people don't believe it. Once you have your basic needs met, more money doesn't equal more happiness. However, money can go a long way toward solving problems and making things easier. It can buy you therapy, books, healers, retreats, and mentors. It can even help you to buy your time back.

YOUR TO-DO LIST WON'T END

Discovering that my to-do list would never end was actually a relief. I realized I wasn't alone: everyone has to-do lists and no one finishes everything on their list every single day—it's simply impossible. Everybody has the exact same panic and fear that they're the only ones who are failing.

If this is something you struggle with, ask people that you know and trust what their to-do list looks like. You might be amazed by how many people open up that they feel as though their to-do list never ends. This kind of perspective is important for all aspects of business, not just your to-do list. Realizing—and remembering—that my standards for myself are so much higher than everyone else's standards for me also really helps me keep the mountain of to-dos at bay.

DREAMS COME TRUE IN UNEXPECTED WAYS

As a kid, I dreamed that I would become a performer, travel around the world, and meet other rock stars. Unfortunately, it turns out I'm not a very good singer. Dream crushed! But I have been able to speak on stages in front of thousands of people. I've met and connected with people who are changing the world. I've been able to meet my business idols, people whose podcasts I've listened to for inspiration. I've even been able to be a guest on a podcast with the biggest audiences in the world. And I've also interviewed some of my heroes, including Robert Greene, one of my all-time favorite authors. My business has allowed me to be a performer—only instead of singing or acting, I'm making presentations, having conversations, and sharing my own wisdom.

Having a successful business has also allowed me to give back to friends and family who helped me. For example, when someone needs a few more bucks to pay a bill, I can fill this need instantly without a second thought. You can literally write that check and solve a problem.

BUSINESS GROWTH GOES HAND IN HAND WITH PERSONAL GROWTH

Running a business is a mirror for your own personal growth and development. In fact, all the problems that come up in your business are going to illuminate things about who you are as a person: how you show up, how you lead, and the parts of you that have to grow. This might not seem like a good thing until you start your personal growth journey and realize the problems that you solve—and how you react to difficult situations—make you stronger.

For example, years ago, if someone was rude to me at the post office, it would mess me up for a day. It would really hurt my feelings. Today, it doesn't bother me. In fact, I can face some pretty tough conversations and confrontations without letting my emotions get the best of me. When I look at my journey, I realize I wouldn't be one-tenth of where I am in my personal growth if it had not been for my business pushing me to the best I could be.

FLEXIBILITY REALLY IS WORTH IT

Being able to set your own schedule is a blessing and a curse. Sometimes you end up working way more than you would if you were working for an employer. However, on the bright side, there's no one around to fire you, and there's no one to tell you what to do. So you get to decide when you work. Do you want to work in the mornings? Do you want to work in the evenings? Do you want to work on weekends? Do you want to work on holidays? Do you want to take four hours off in the middle of the day to go get your nails done or read a book at a café? You can do whatever you want when you build your own business, and to me that flexibility is worth it.

TAKEAWAYS

- *Journal:* Choose one of the points from this chapter to journal about. What surprises you about it? What do you find intimidating? What do you find exciting? What do you have questions about?

- *Reflect:* What are the good and bad surprises, benefits and perks, and unexpected insights you've learned on your business journey so far? What are some surprising things you've learned from this book?

- *Do:* Choose a mind-training technique such as meditation or affirmations. Do some research on how to go about this technique, then find space in your routine for a week or month to give it a try.

CHAPTER 21

Creating Bigger Goals

Wishes and goals help you visualize where you want your life and business to go in the future. The two ideas are related: a wish is when you have a dream and you say, "I really hope that this happens." A goal offers something more concrete—a specific end point. A goal is also something you've identified that's within reach, and you've taken at least one action step to make it a reality. In fact, creating a list of action steps is a great way to help you start moving forward to achieve a goal.

As your business grows, you'll want to set bigger goals for yourself, both in the short term (goals for this week or this month) and in the long term (this year, next year, and even 5 to 10 years in the future). Are you looking to grow your clients? Are you determining strategy around a new product launch? Do you want to give a speech at a conference? No goal is ever guaranteed, of course, but being intentional about what you want to achieve can at the very least increase the chances of it happening.

SEVEN-FIGURE BUSINESS OWNERS

Maybe one of your goals is to become a seven-figure business owner. As we discussed in Chapter 2, five- and six-figure businesses are very similar. What it takes to be a seven-figure earner—a business owner—is completely different. You need to change the way you look at work, the way you look at your business, the way you operate, and the way you show up. It's very difficult to work hard enough to get to seven figures without a complete reinvention of everything you've learned before and who you are. What worked for you to get to six figures isn't going to work here. You have to reinvent your systems and switch up everything from communication approach to leadership style. There's way less wiggle room for mistakes as a seven-figure business owner.

However, going to seven figures is not always going to be right for everyone, and it's certainly not right for everyone at every time in their life. Maybe you're homeschooling your kids or taking care of a family member who is chronically ill. You have to know what season you're in in order to determine whether right now is the best time to pursue seven figures.

NOW WHAT?

What nobody really tells you is that once you hit your initial goals, you're going to feel super empty. You've worked so hard to reach big milestones—and now you have to figure out what's next. As your business becomes more successful, better goals—or next-level goals—are really important to define.

One of the best ways to start creating next-level goals is to gain inspiration from people who you admire. I really like the approach by Evan Carmichael, who teaches the concept #believenation via his YouTube channel. Drawing on interviews from successful people such as Oprah Winfrey and Steve Jobs, he has put together videos that are full of life lessons and rules for success. When thinking about this, try to stretch your mind beyond what seems immediately obvious. I tap into my childhood dreams as well as browse magazines, Pinterest, and Zillow.

Once, I heard business adviser and change management expert Price Pritchett say: "If everything went according to plan, if I knew I couldn't fail, what would I go for?" That's the big question to consider when setting next-level goals.

COMMON NEXT-LEVEL GOALS

Next-level goals could be changing your life blueprint, or how you're living by design.

Next-level goals could also involve having a positive impact on other people's lives. For example, if you find yourself hitting a monetary goal and wondering what's next, ask yourself, "What problems in this world could I solve with my ability to generate this resource? What do people need?" If you're interested in having an impact this way, it's important to listen to what's going on in your community. Listen to people in the community and meet the needs that they are requesting instead of coming up with what you think will meet their needs.

So, one next-level goal could be a funding a nonprofit. I personally dream of finding ways to create sustainable farms and housing or of creating a fund dedicated to providing diaper and feminine hygiene products to people who need them. I would love to be able to support single mothers and people who are experiencing homelessness by offering education and practical assistance so that they're equipped with the right skills when applying for a job or opportunities. It all begins with a dream.

THERE IS NO EASY BUTTON

Getting to the point where you're setting bigger goals takes patience and dedication—and there are no shortcuts. I spent a lot more time than I'm comfortable admitting to searching for some secret about easy business growth that I was missing. I was hoping to chance upon something like, "Oh, here's this 1-2-3 step system that will allow you to have success faster." I searched so hard and even spent tons of money on big promises and discovered that no easy button exists. If it did, trust me—I would have found it by now!

Everyone who is trying to sell some version of an easy button is selling you a promise of gold at the end of the rainbow. There's not some magical productivity routine that applies to everyone or every business. Everybody's path to success looks different and takes different amounts of time. This is why I've broken down different tactics throughout this book for work, study, and business, and personal growth habits that are simple to implement without spending tons of money.

Of course, we can study the habits and patterns of successful people and sometimes find useful shortcuts or tips. We can implement the things that successful people do and learn from their mistakes. But following someone else's system is no guarantee of success.

The side effect of doing things right—although, yes, it is hard—is that you'll accomplish more faster than those who spend their lives looking for the easy button. I know now that I prefer to do hard things any day because that work can help me build a life that is easy.

DON'T SKIP THE BASICS

In addition to looking for an easy button, people are often looking for some magical answer about how they can skip the basics of running a business. These basics include:

1. Getting visible—in other words, making sure people know that you exist
2. Generating leads
3. Closing sales
4. Delivering with excellence
5. Retention and referral
6. Upselling

Once, someone wanted to leave one of my programs because they thought that everything being presented was very basic—there weren't any mind-blowing revelations. I remember asking them, "Well, have you applied this basic info to your own life? Have you applied what you've learned so far to your business?" Their answer was no, in fact, they hadn't. Basics are basic for a reason. More often than not, people try to jump ahead and they miss some of those foundational steps. Take these examples:

"Rachel, how did you write a book?"
Me: "I opened a Word document and started typing."

"Rachel, how did you get fit?"
Me: "I ate more vegetables, drank water, and worked out regularly."

"Rachel, how do you and Poul maintain your marriage?"
Me: "We commit, we communicate, and we try to connect each and every day."

People are sometimes annoyed when I ask them, "Did you start with the simple and basic ideas?" But that's often my best advice because sometimes we overcomplicate the things that are very, very simple. For example, if you're working with five clients right now, and you want to double your business, the simple solution is to take on five more clients. If you are happy with the types of leads that you currently get but you want to turn it up by 10 percent, you should do 10 percent more of the activities that are generating leads.

People are willing to put in so much work to try to find shortcuts or bypass foundational steps. They could be spending that time just getting the basics done! Great things are built from a series of small action steps. In fact, whenever things start to feel too complicated, there's a good chance that you've gotten away from the basics. However, the truth is, "the people who are advanced just never don't do the basics. They always do them," as Alex Hormozi, the founder of Gym Launch, has said:

> When compounded over years, the basics are what create consistency, a rock-solid foundation, and an excellent reputation. The basics are what generate referrals and keep customers coming back, offering you the ability to grow your company and offer more.

TAKEAWAYS

- *Journal:* What are your current goals? What kind of impact do you want your business to have in the future? What do you see as your bigger, long-term goals? How are these different from your current goals? Do they reflect one another?

- *Reflect:* Are you bypassing the basics? What kinds of foundational steps can you lean back into?

- *Do:* After journaling about your dream, write it on a sticky note and put it somewhere you will see it all the time. It's never too early to focus on your dreams!

CHAPTER 22

Why Choose?

One night after a live event, my team and the speakers went out to dinner. We ended up at one of my favorite places, and everybody was telling stories, laughing, and having a great time. As we neared the end of our dinner, the most impossible situation came about. They brought out the dessert menu, and I saw *two* of my favorite desserts: tiramisu and crème brûlée. I felt existential dread take over my mind. I am a huge fan of dessert and have a mega sweet tooth. As a kid, I would beg my parents (unsuccessfully) for two bowls of ice cream after dinner, and I've polished off an entire package of Oreos in one sitting.

My friend Stacey caught me looking concerned and said, "Sweetie, what's wrong?" I explained to her that I wanted both the tiramisu and the crème brûlée. Stacey burst out laughing. Apparently, she had been worried that something had seriously gone wrong. "Why choose?" she said. "Get them both."

I was so stressed about what to choose I almost didn't pick either one. It didn't even occur to me that getting both was an option. But I did order both desserts, had a couple of bites of each (okay, maybe more like two-thirds of each), and everyone else got to take a bite of the sweets I'd ordered along with their own desserts.

In my business life, I've also experienced the same dilemma of deliberating between two amazing options and not realizing that both might be possible.

YOU ARE A BEAUTIFUL PARADOX

I've also run into people who didn't understand or respect that I might be filling multiple roles. Take the time I was flying to an event in Nashville. While sitting in the exit row, I heard a man speaking to the flight attendant about me.

Man: She might not be strong enough to assist with an emergency.

Me (indignantly turning around): I've had three babies. I'm strong.

Man: You're not old enough to have three kids.

Me: I'll take that as a compliment . . . But I do—so here we are.

Man: You're traveling, though—so you must not get much time with them.

Excuse me? This man was rudely underestimating and judging me, and he also didn't realize that you can choose multiple paths and rock them all in different ways. Do I want to be a mom? Or do I want to be a business owner? Trick question: it's not a binary option! You can do both as long as you understand the hard work and occasional priority shifting that it requires.

For example, when I'm in a busy work season, you better believe my kids are going to be eating more frozen pizzas and lasagnas with a side of steamed broccoli from the microwave. Certain sacrifices have to be made.

Every path we might choose in life has its own rewards and challenges. Though this book is filtered through my experience as a woman in business who has three children and a husband, women whose main jobs are being mothers or those who focus on a career instead of having kids are choosing equally valid and equally challenging paths. There is an unfortunate and persistent narrative in our culture that tells people—and women especially—that they have to choose a lane, and that there are certain expectations about what they can and can't do.

But here's what people often overlook about women. We are incredibly multifaceted. We are walking, talking contradictions. Call us beautiful paradoxes—yet we can do many different things in a single lifetime, flowing from parent to coach to salesperson to athlete, all in one afternoon.

We can be powerful businesswomen and loving mothers.

We can be strong and sensitive.

We can be silly and serious.

We can be joyful and full of grief at the same time.

We can be sexy and nurturing.

Maybe you've heard the saying that someone who has many responsibilities wears a lot of hats? I prefer to think that most of the women I know wear a lot of shoes. You can flip between shoes up to 10 times a day, each time assuming a completely different identity. Some shoes are for running, some are for comfort, some are for date night, some are just cute. We don't need to choose just one pair!

FIND THE RESET

What's so wonderful about coming into a new week is that it gives you the chance to reset. You get to slam that reset button and say, "Yes, we're going to crush this week. It's going to be amazing. I'm going to have time for everything that's important to me. I'm going to get my priorities done first thing every day and hammer through them."

And the beautiful thing is, you can choose to do this every single day, not just Monday. You can go to bed and say, "Tomorrow, I get to wake up a new person. A new creation, a new leader, a new partner. I get to show up 110 percent. I don't have to let the guilt or shame of the past affect me."

Every single day is also a chance to slam that reset button and say, "Yesterday does not matter. The only thing that matters today is here. Today is a brand-new day."

TAKE AN INVENTORY OF YOUR TIME

Have you ever heard someone say, "We all have the same 24 hours every day," or "Beyoncé only has 24 hours in a day," or "Billionaires have the same amount of time each day as we do"?

I have heard those things and literally rolled my eyes. I have three kids, but no personal trainer or private chef. It would be easy to achieve what celebrities and billionaires do if I had loads of money, a massive team, and all the opportunities to make my life more seamless. But let's be real for a moment: I barely have time to wash my hair and make a dinner that the whole family likes. I can't worry about using my 24 hours like Oprah Winfrey, because I am not Oprah Winfrey.

But one day, something clicked in my head. What if we have it backward?

What if Beyoncé doesn't manage her time wisely because she's Beyoncé? What if Beyoncé *became* Beyoncé because she manages her time wisely?

What if The Rock doesn't work out regularly because he's The Rock? What if The Rock *became* The Rock because he works out regularly?

This realization forever changed the way I saw cause and effect. As a result, I decided to do an inventory of my personal time outside of building my business. I knew that I was working 45–55 hours a week. But where was my free time going? Here's what my time inventory revealed:

Monday–Friday:

8 a.m.: Slowly waking up, scrolling TikTok, sipping coffee, being cranky

9 a.m.: Doing makeup on a TikTok Live slowly

9:30 a.m.–6:30 p.m.: Working

6:30 p.m.: Scrolling TikTok

7 p.m.: Family dinner and sometimes a game

8 p.m.: Watching random YouTube videos

8:30 p.m.: Bedtime routines for the kids

9:30 p.m.: Watching TV shows to unwind while playing Toon Blast on my phone

1 a.m.: Fall asleep

Saturday–Sunday:

9 a.m.–1 a.m.: Errands, watching TV and movies, playing with the kids for two to five hours per day, lying around "relaxing"

What I found in this time study felt like a punch to the gut. I was spending a ton of time each day browsing, scrolling, and mindlessly wasting *hours*. From Monday to Friday,

I found six hours of "hidden time" per day. *Thirty hours a week*?! And then there were the weekends, where I uncovered two to five hours of hidden time per day. Just by adding a little intention and awareness, I discovered between 34 and 40 hours of total hidden time *per week*. On top of that, I realized I wasn't even spending much time with my husband or my family.

After the time inventory, coupled with the intentionality of time blocking, I realized how the celebrities became who they wanted to be. They had better time management skills—and used their free time wisely.

So I took a look at my wish list:

I wanted to write a book.

I wanted to speak French, Russian, and Chinese.

I wanted to play the cello.

I wanted to have a garden.

I wanted to run a marathon.

I wanted to learn how to code.

And, with my new time, I started tackling these things. I started writing 200 to 2,000 words per day.

I replaced Toon Blast on my phone each evening with Duolingo. As a result, I became lightly conversational in French in just 16 months!

I got a cello and started taking weekly lessons on Saturdays for 30 minutes.

I spent a weekend with the kids planting an indoor garden, mostly vegetable plants!

I started running three to four miles several times a week, with the goal of running a marathon.

I haven't started coding yet, but it's coming soon!

I practically doubled my useable week. As it turns out, I do have the same amount of time as Beyoncé in a given week—I just needed to repurpose how I was using it. On top of these new activities, I blocked out extra time for family time. Poul and I go on dates or just spend time connecting, I do fun hairstyles for the girls in the mornings, and the time I spend with the kids on the weekends is actually quality time.

HOW TO PRIORITIZE

I hate when people call me busy. Busy says to me, "I am trying to find importance in doing a lot of things." It doesn't say to me, "This is a confident person who has learned how to prioritize and not be apologetic when some things don't fit."

I prefer to say, "I have time for everything that is a priority to me."

Deciding your priorities is crucial. I like to write down no more than six priorities in a given season. Let's say I write down business, spirituality, self-care, my family, friendship, and my fitness. Then, cross out two. This is how you know that you are really serious about the four that are left. These are the non-negotiable things in your life, and, at least for this season, they will be the main focus.

Now, you want to place them in order of importance to help guide your decisions. For example, if my top priorities are my family, my business, and my friends, everything else takes a back seat. Then, if my girlfriends were to say, "Hey,

Rachel, do you want to go on a weeklong trip?" I would say, "You know what, I would love to, but the kids are young. That's just not a priority for me right now. But if you want to keep asking, please do—because maybe someday it will work out and we'll all be able to go." If there's a weeklong trip for business, I have to ask myself, how's the family doing? Do we feel like there's some balance there? And if the answer's no, it's just going to have to be a no. But if there's maybe a three-day trip, and I say okay, I can do that without it interrupting my family's schedule.

There are some people who say you can only have one priority in life, but I don't agree with that. I really think that there's a little bit of a hierarchy, though it may change depending on the season.

TAKEAWAYS

- *Journal:* What does the sentiment "why choose?" make you think of? How does it make you feel? Where are the areas in your life where you might not have to choose? How can you make that happen?

- *Reflect:* What are your current priorities? How do they rank? Is there anything you thought was a priority that isn't getting the time it deserves?

- *Do:* Make an inventory of your personal time outside of building your business to help you identify places where you're being unproductive and secure more free time.

CHAPTER 23

When You Feel Like Giving Up . . .

When you feel like giving up, this chapter is for you. Maybe save this chapter for that day, or read it in advance, or read it every single time you need it. When it feels like everything's falling apart, when the world has turned against you, when your family and friends don't understand your dreams, I have words of truth and encouragement for you.

I've spent a lifetime doubting myself and my success. I spent far too long not being sure if I could make it. Then I spent forever feeling like maybe my success wasn't meant for me. Maybe it was actually meant for my sister, my best friend, or my neighbor. Maybe the dream was meant for someone more qualified or conventional. I'm too normal. I'm not fit. I don't have a six-pack. I'm not a person who's five-foot-ten in high heels and sashays across stages with the beautiful grace of a corporate speaker.

After a lifetime of doubting myself, I decided it was time for me to try something else: believing that I am worthy and capable, and that I'm meant to be on any stage, heels or no.

Giving yourself permission to believe in yourself is powerful. And you're going to be amazed by how quickly things can shift. If what you have thought and believed up until now has led you to a place you don't want to be, change the script. If you want to end up somewhere else, this is the opportunity for you to try something different. It's time to switch up your mindset. If doubt isn't working, why not try belief?

Now, we all have patterns. Maybe you're thinking, *Oh, I don't have a routine, I don't have habits, I don't have patterns.* But you've definitely created patterns without even realizing it. Even the lack of habits and routines is a pattern. You might resist or be afraid of adding something different, or even taking away some of the bad patterns. Change can be hard and scary! But the patterns you're following right now are either currently getting you the results you want—or they're not. Simple as that. And this goes double for your day-to-day work. The way you approach social media, the way that you show up for your business, the way that you're working with clients—all those things are either currently getting you the desired results, or they're not.

So if you want something different than what your current patterns and habits are creating, let them go. And let your old beliefs go too. Both need to change. If you only change your desire for a different outcome, the old habits will hold you down. Don't spend your entire life chasing something you'll never catch—you have so much to offer.

THE POWER OF PERCEPTION

One way to start changing your life is by embracing the power of perception. Through studying marketing, I learned that perception is reality. In order to create your desired perception of a product, service, or situation, you need to create several indications that the desired perception is true. Then the rest of the dots will begin to fill in.

I decided to test this theory about the power of perception and see what would happen in relation to my *self-confidence.*

I turned this into a full-on experiment. I wanted to be perceived as a confident person, so I began to study the patterns of people I admired. As I studied tons of confident people, I discovered many of them had similar traits:

- They stood tall, no matter their height.
- They wore their clothing unapologetically.
- They seemed to have their own style that didn't necessarily fit the current fashion.
- They spoke in a way that commanded attention.
- No matter how loudly or quietly they spoke, they never seemed to waver.
- They didn't apologize for existing (unless they hurt someone).
- They made others feel okay about being themselves.
- They seem genuinely okay with who they were.

I followed their lead. I stood tall, wore my clothes with intention, and followed the other behaviors I had observed. Suddenly, I started closing bigger deals—deals worth thousands (and even hundreds of thousands!) of dollars. Huge events started contacting me and asking me to speak on their stages: 100 people, 1,000 people, 5,000 people, 12,000 people! Big brands such as American Express and Square e-mailed me and asked me to partner with them on big projects.

I was absolutely blown away. The only change I made was adopting the mannerisms of a *successful* person, and so many good things started to follow.

YOU'RE NOT ALONE

Of course, shifting your perception doesn't happen overnight. In general, it's hard to make changes, much less admit you need to change. And changes take time to take hold.

There have been so many times where I have turned off the computer at the end of the day and thought, *I can't take any more. I can't handle this. I can't do this. God, you've got the wrong girl again.* There are days when you too might start to wonder, *Was this even worth it? What am I thinking? Am I crazy? This can't happen for me.*

I've been there. And I know what it's like to be at the depths of your journey and wondering whether it's going to pay off; whether your dreams were really just hallucinations; whether you're tough enough, pretty enough, competent enough. I know what you're going through because I have been there. I want to let you know the words that I needed someone to tell me when I went through that season. All I wanted was for someone to tell me, "Sweet girl, you are not alone. And, yes, all of this is totally normal."

In the season when everything feels like it's falling apart, you're going to discover how much you believe in what you do. In the season when no one else understands what you want to build, you'll believe even more strongly in this thing that's bigger than life. In the season when no one else can do what you're doing, you will find your true voice for the first time.

That is the time when you have to dig deep and develop new skills. You'll discover newfound grit, an ability to push through when you feel like everything is collapsing around you. Your legs will get stronger from picking yourself up over and over and over again. Your back will become a shield as you learn to protect yourself from people shooting arrows of doubt and fear at you. This last part is difficult because often what others say mirrors the exact doubts inside your head.

Yet in those moments, where I'm in a weak and broken place and get back up again after thinking I can't handle more, I discover the real strength running through my core. And you have it too. We're all stronger than we know. Every single successful person has felt unworthy at some point. Every other person who has created something huge has wondered, *Everything's falling apart, will this ever pay off?* They've had those moments where they cried in their car or hid in the closet because they didn't want anyone else to see that they were falling apart. You too might feel as though you have to be strong for everyone else. It's okay to cry. It's okay to journal. It's okay to feel all the things intensely and to doubt and to wonder if you're the wrong person to make this dream come to life.

Putting yourself back in the ring and choosing to go another round when things feel hopeless is difficult, but it is possible. And it's probably going to look different than how you imagined—and, yes, it is a lot less glamorous than anyone ever tells you. But the journey is what makes you the person who can stand up and be capable of taking on bigger responsibilities.

The responsibilities don't ever end. You don't ever hit a point in your career or in your business where you say, "Well, thank goodness, I've made it. All right, it's all taken care of now." The challenges get stronger and bigger. Just like a video game, every single level is more and more challenging, and you have to develop and refine your skill set accordingly. I know what you are going through right now is tough.

But a year from now—or 3, 5, or even 10 years—you'll look back and say, "Wow, that was nothing. Look at how strong I am today. Look at how far I've come—and look at how standing back up and showing back up and putting my voice back out there made a difference. Look how my resilience and my grit and my determination and my belief were developed in those toughest moments."

You're not alone, you are absolutely capable of doing this.

So get back up one more time. You don't have to imagine anything else any further in the future. Look at just this moment square in the face. Believe in yourself and be determined to try one more time.

And before you know it, you're not trying anymore. You're doing it.

BEFORE AND AFTER PICTURES

If you're anything like me, you may look at your current self as a series of before pictures. These are photos that show someone who's a work in progress, not where (or *who*) they want to be, both in business and life. In the past, here's how I've talked about myself:

I want to speak seven languages, but I don't . . .

I want to write a book, but I haven't . . .

I want to run a marathon, but I've never run more than 11 miles . . .

I'm not fit . . .

I'm not able to play the instruments I want to play . . .

I'm not good at remembering birthdays . . .

I'm renting, not in my forever home . . .

Looking at our lives as before pictures keeps us in a cycle of shame and frustration. After all, it's easy to beat yourself up and feel as though you're always behind everyone else and not as successful as other people. Staying in this mindset keeps us from continually growing.

I know this feeling, but it's important to remember that you do not exist just to be a before picture. I'm not just talking about your physical appearance—I'm talking about every area of your life. In order to move forward, we have to acknowledge how much we've grown.

Today is a point on a long journey. Think about how far you've come already, and celebrate the progress you've made over the last 3, 10, and even 20 years. Take a moment and acknowledge that today is both a before picture and an after picture. We get so focused on considering all that we haven't accomplished, we forget to give ourselves credit for the fact that we've already come quite far. And you deserve credit for that growth and healing.

Take my own situation. A decade ago, I was a single mom with major debt from medical bills, credit cards, and student loans. I was a volatile person in relationships. I was a sobbing, crying mess every single night, feeling like a total failure. I wasn't healthy in any way. A decade later, I now:

. . . *speak three languages.*

. . . *can curl 15-pound dumbbells!*

. . . *bought a cello, so I'm a step closer to playing it.*

. . . *remember my family members' birthdays.*

. . . *have a spacious home that fits my family's needs.*

. . . *wrote a book!*

A powerful way to change your relationship between the present (what currently is) and the future (what you desire to happen) is to add one simple word: *yet.*

This word changes the entire game by reminding you that the present moment is another progress-filled point in your journey. It can be tacked on to all your before statements to change your relationship with these words. This allows an opening for growth, it gives you credit for the progress you've made, and it helps you realize the beautiful power of the current moment.

I want to speak seven languages, but I don't . . . yet.

I want to write a book, but I haven't . . . yet.

I want to run a marathon, but I've never run more than 11 miles . . . yet.

I'm not fit . . . yet.

I'm not able to play the instruments I want to play . . . yet.

I'm not good at remembering birthdays . . . yet.

I'm not in my forever home . . . yet.

Without "yet," those statements only show your life as a series of before pictures. By adding it, you're opening your life to possibility, forward movement, and change. This is what transforms the future and allows you to continually evolve and reach your potential—freeing yourself from stagnancy, shame, and frustration.

EMBRACE GRATITUDE

People who are committed to growth always want a better tomorrow. That's why we're so excited when the calendar flips over at midnight on New Year's Eve—it's a fresh start. However, the number-one thing that you can do to ensure a better tomorrow—if not a better year and a better decade—is to embrace everything that's good about today. You have a choice to be grateful for every single thing in your life today.

Be grateful for your clients.

Be grateful for the progress you've made.

Be thankful for the people in your life.

Be thankful for your friendships.

Be grateful for your marriage.

Be grateful for the roof over your head.

Be grateful for the food you have available.

Be grateful for the amount in your bank account.

When you focus too much on the things you want—instead of what you have—it feels like you're chasing a mirage that's always getting further away.

For example, I see so many people chasing the next relationship because they're not in their dream relationship. But when you look at your spouse and say, "Oh my gosh, I am so thankful for you. You are the love of my life. You are the dream that I've had," your current relationship will blossom. When you start to be grateful for the friendships that you have, and say, "Wow, I'm so glad that I'm blessed with incredible people in my life," your existing relationships will become deeper.

Just remember: if you aren't grateful for what's here today and only focus on the things that you want in the future, what you're waiting on will never arrive. Your business will serve you as long as you continually care about serving your business and customers today.

TAKEAWAYS

- *Journal:* How can you embrace gratitude? Incorporate a gratitude practice in your daily journaling. When you finish writing, jot down five specific things that you're grateful for. It could be the sound of the birds singing outside, the fact that your partner made you breakfast, that you had a meeting and really crushed it. Anything at all!

- *Reflect:* Consider how often you take what you perceive as being reality. What kinds of assumptions do you make about others based on the way they look or act? What kinds of assumptions have been made about you?

- *Do:* Choose a habit or routine—perhaps it's your morning routine or what you do when you first sit down at the computer to work. Look at how you spend your time and what kind of mindset you're in. How can you shift your routines so what you do is more aligned with your goals?

Afterword

Starting a business is one of the top five best decisions I've made in my life. I'm not trying to convince you to start a business, I promise. Chances are you picked up this book because it's been a thought in the back of your mind. The thing I underestimated about business is that it's not a "one and done" choice. I thought it was something that you just picked, like a hair color: "Yay, I'm an entrepreneur now!" No. It's a decision that you need to choose over and over and over.

In no particular order, the top five best decisions I've made in my life:

1. Marrying Poul.
2. Having our kids.
3. Going sober.
4. Choosing God.
5. Starting a business.

With each one of these things on this list, I make a conscious effort to choose them on a daily basis.

I married Poul, but we have to choose commitment every day.

I have three kids, but I have to choose to be a participating mom every day.

I got sober, but I have to choose to stay sober each day.

I follow God, but I have to choose to continue following and seeking every day.

I started a business, but I have to choose to be a business owner every day.

I'm able to make these choices every day because I've built strong business boundaries and have a supportive family and team around me. The truth is, we all need someone to believe in us. If you have never had that person (or the only person has been your mom or your husband, and you don't feel like that counts), the next words are for you.

Imagine in this moment that you and I are sitting down for dinner. Suddenly I reach across the table and hold your hand. I look you in the eyes and tell you the unfiltered truth—what you deserve to hear.

Beautiful girl, they were all wrong about you.

You did what you had to do to get through those times.

You have permission to go after your dreams now.

Your dreams matter.

You owe it to the younger version of yourself to go after them.

You owe it to the future version of yourself to leave no stone unturned.

Show the world that you are not done dreaming, that your dreams are valid.

Do something with those beautiful dreams.

I'm here for you, and don't ever forget it.

But in case no one has told you lately, I see your potential.

You were made for this.

Okay, are you ready? Let's go.

Index

Acknowledgments

To my husband and partner, Poul. You were the first person who showed me that I was worthy of love—completely unfiltered. To my assistant and sister-like friend, Kellyanne, for keeping me on schedule, keeping me from burnout, and keeping me going. To my family and family-in-law, I couldn't have written this book without your support. Truly. To my friends for loving me even though I do some crazy things. To Russell Brunson for telling me to write a book and supporting me for years. To Annie Grace for being an amazing friend when I was crying and voxing you every chapter of the way. To Louise Hay for inspiring me endlessly. To Hay House, Reid Tracy, Anne Barthel, Patty Gift, and the entire team. To my collaborative writer, Annie Zaleski, for helping my ADHD writing become something readable. To my team, who keeps everything going. To Kary Oberbrunner, Rachel Miller, Bart Miller, Molly Mahoney, Krista Mashore, John and Jeanne Buttolph, Myron Golden, and Peng Joon for all being so supportive and inspiring. To the incredibly talented members of The Social Clique—who amaze me more each day.

About the Author

Rachel Pedersen is CEO of an award-winning international digital marketing agency and founder of Social Media United, the leading online education center for social media managers. As a full-time social media consultant and strategist, she empowers business owners and social media managers to leverage social media and fast-track their growth trajectories. With her husband, Poul, who's also her business partner and COO, she is raising three children and supporting thousands of students and clients and millions more fans and followers on the amazing journey of entrepreneurship—helping them find freedom and joy along the way.

Website: RachelPedersen.com

Hay House Titles of Related Interest

We hope you enjoyed this Hay House book. If you'd like to receive our online catalog featuring additional information on Hay House books and products, or if you'd like to find out more about the Hay Foundation, please contact:

Hay House, Inc., P.O. Box 5100, Carlsbad, CA 92018-5100
(760) 431-7695 or (800) 654-5126
(760) 431-6948 (fax) or (800) 650-5115 (fax)
www.hayhouse.com® • www.hayfoundation.org

———

Published in Australia by: Hay House Australia Pty. Ltd.,
18/36 Ralph St., Alexandria NSW 2015
Phone: 612-9669-4299 • *Fax:* 612-9669-4144
www.hayhouse.com.au

Published in the United Kingdom by: Hay House UK, Ltd.,
The Sixth Floor, Watson House, 54 Baker Street, London W1U 7BU
Phone: +44 (0)20 3927 7290 • *Fax:* +44 (0)20 3927 7291
www.hayhouse.co.uk

Published in India by: Hay House Publishers India,
Muskaan Complex, Plot No. 3, B-2, Vasant Kunj, New Delhi 110 070
Phone: 91-11-4176-1620 • *Fax:* 91-11-4176-1630
www.hayhouse.co.in

———

Access New Knowledge.
Anytime. Anywhere.

Learn and evolve at your own pace
with the world's leading experts.

www.hayhouseU.com

TIME FOR RACHEL TO GIVE.

TIME FOR YOU TO RECEIVE.

Rachel is honored you've read the book.
She wants to pour on the value.

RACHEL WANTS TO CONNECT WITH YOU.

Rachel Pedersen is an expert in all things social media.

Follow her on your favorite social media platforms and get the clarity you crave.

RachelPedersen.com